An Analysis of

Robert E. Lucas Jr.'s

Why Doesn't Capital Flow from Rich to Poor Countries?

Pádraig Belton

Published by Macat International Ltd
24:13 Coda Centre, 189 Munster Road, London SW6 6AW.

Distributed exclusively by Routledge
2 Park Square, Milton Park, Abingdon, Oxon OX14 4RN
711 Third Avenue, New York, NY 10017, USA

Routledge is an imprint of the Taylor & Francis Group, an informa business

www.macat.com
info@macat.com

Cataloguing in Publication Data
A catalogue record for this book is available from the British Library.
Library of Congress Cataloguing-in-Publication Data is available upon request.
Cover illustration: Etienne Gilfillan

ISBN 978-1-912302-27-7 (hardback)
ISBN 978-1-912128-43-3 (paperback)
ISBN 978-1-912281-15-2 (e-book)

Notice

The information in this book is designed to orientate readers of the work under analysis,
to elucidate and contextualise its key ideas and themes, and to aid in the development
of critical thinking skills. It is not meant to be used, nor should it be used, as a
substitute for original thinking or in place of original writing or research. References and
notes are provided for informational purposes and their presence does not constitute
endorsement of the information or opinions therein. This book is presented solely for
educational purposes. It is sold on the understanding that the publisher is not engaged
to provide any scholarly advice. The publisher has made every effort to ensure that
this book is accurate and up-to-date, but makes no warranties or representations with
regard to the completeness or reliability of the information it contains. The information
and the opinions provided herein are not guaranteed or warranted to produce particular
results and may not be suitable for students of every ability. The publisher shall not be
liable for any loss, damage or disruption arising from any errors or omissions, or from
the use of this book, including, but not limited to, special, incidental, consequential or
other damages caused, or alleged to have been caused, directly or indirectly, by the
information contained within.

CONTENTS

THE MACAT LIBRARY

The Macat Library is a series of unique academic explorations of seminal works in the humanities and social sciences – books and papers that have had a significant and widely recognised impact on their disciplines. It has been created to serve as much more than just a summary of what lies between the covers of a great book. It illuminates and explores the influences on, ideas of, and impact of that book. Our goal is to offer a learning resource that encourages critical thinking and fosters a better, deeper understanding of important ideas.

Each publication is divided into three Sections: Influences, Ideas, and Impact. Each Section has four Modules. These explore every important facet of the work, and the responses to it.

This Section-Module structure makes a Macat Library book easy to use, but it has another important feature. Because each Macat book is written to the same format, it is possible (and encouraged!) to cross-reference multiple Macat books along the same lines of inquiry or research. This allows the reader to open up interesting interdisciplinary pathways.

To further aid your reading, lists of glossary terms and people mentioned are included at the end of this book (these are indicated by an asterisk [*] throughout) – as well as a list of works cited.

Macat has worked with the University of Cambridge to identify the elements of critical thinking and understand the ways in which six different skills combine to enable effective thinking.
Three allow us to fully understand a problem; three more give us the tools to solve it. Together, these six skills make up the **PACIER** model of critical thinking. They are:

ANALYSIS – understanding how an argument is built
EVALUATION – exploring the strengths and weaknesses of an argument
INTERPRETATION – understanding issues of meaning

CREATIVE THINKING – coming up with new ideas and fresh connections
PROBLEM-SOLVING – producing strong solutions
REASONING – creating strong arguments

To find out more, visit **WWW.MACAT.COM.**

CRITICAL THINKING AND "WHY DOESN'T CAPITAL FLOW FROM RICH TO POOR COUNTRIES?"

Primary critical thinking skill: PROBLEM SOLVING
Secondary critical thinking skill: REASONING

Robert Lucas is known among economists as one of the most influential macroeconomists of recent times – a reputation founded in no small part on the critical thinking skills displayed in his seminal 1990 paper 'Why Doesn't Capital Flow from Rich to Poor Countries?'

Lucas's paper tackles a puzzle in economic theory that has since come to be known as the 'Lucas paradox,' and it deploys the author's brilliant problem solving skills to explain why such an apparent paradox in fact makes sense. Classical economic theory makes a simple prediction of how capital flows between countries: it should, it states, flow from rich to poor countries, because of the law of diminishing returns on capital. Since poor countries have so little capital invested in them, the returns on new investment should be proportionally far better than investment in rich countries.

This should mean that investors seeking new opportunities will invest in poorer countries, making capital consistently flow from rich nations to poorer ones. But, problematically, this is not in fact the case. Having defined the problem, Lucas did what any good problem solver would: he looked critically at the criteria involved, and offered a series of possible solutions. Indeed, in just six pages, he puts forward four hypotheses to explain the paradox's existence. The popularity of his paper, and the influence it has had, are also greatly magnified by careful reasoning embodied in Lucas's marshalling of evidence and his explanations of the judgements he has made.

ABOUT THE AUTHOR OF THE ORIGINAL WORK

Born in 1937, **Robert E. Lucas Jr.** is an economics professor at the University of Chicago. While at school he used mathematical theories to solve a design problem for his father's business, reinforcing his passion for the subject. Lucas won the Nobel Prize in Economics in 1995 for his research into how people use 'rational expectations' to make decisions based on all the information available to them. He is probably best known for his 1990 article 'Why Doesn't Capital Flow from Rich to Poor Countries?' which showed, with typical mathematical rigor, that the quantity of capital that does flow between nations is far smaller than accepted economic principles predict.

ABOUT THE AUTHOR OF THE ANALYSIS

Pádraig Belton is completing his doctoral research in politics and international relations at the University of Oxford. A prolific financial, business and political journalist, his work has appeared in publications including the *Irish Times,* the *Guardian, Telegraph, Independent,* the *Irish Independent, The Atlantic, the New Statesman, Prospect, the Times Literary Supplement,* and *Foreign Policy,* as well as via the BBC.

ABOUT MACAT

GREAT WORKS FOR CRITICAL THINKING

Macat is focused on making the ideas of the world's great thinkers accessible and comprehensible to everybody, everywhere, in ways that promote the development of enhanced critical thinking skills.

It works with leading academics from the world's top universities to produce new analyses that focus on the ideas and the impact of the most influential works ever written across a wide variety of academic disciplines. Each of the works that sit at the heart of its growing library is an enduring example of great thinking. But by setting them in context – and looking at the influences that shaped their authors, as well as the responses they provoked – Macat encourages readers to look at these classics and game-changers with fresh eyes. Readers learn to think, engage and challenge their ideas, rather than simply accepting them.

"Macat offers an amazing first-of-its-kind tool for interdisciplinary learning and research. Its focus on works that transformed their disciplines and its rigorous approach, drawing on the world's leading experts and educational institutions, opens up a world-class education to anyone."

Andreas Schleicher
Director for Education and Skills, Organisation for Economic
Co-operation and Development

'Macat is taking on some of the major challenges in university education ... They have drawn together a strong team of active academics who are producing teaching materials that are novel in the breadth of their approach.'

Prof Lord Broers,
former Vice-Chancellor of the University of Cambridge

'The Macat vision is exceptionally exciting. It focuses upon new modes of learning which analyse and explain seminal texts which have profoundly influenced world thinking and so social and economic development. It promotes the kind of critical thinking which is essential for any society and economy. This is the learning of the future.'

Rt Hon Charles Clarke, former UK Secretary of State for Education

'The Macat analyses provide immediate access to the critical conversation surrounding the books that have shaped their respective discipline, which will make them an invaluable resource to all of those, students and teachers, working in the field.'

Professor William Tronzo, University of California at San Diego

WAYS IN TO THE TEXT

KEY POINTS

- According to widely accepted economic theory, capital* —
  that is, money—should flow from wealthier regions to
  poorer ones as long as there is a lower level of capital
  invested per worker in poorer regions and a potential for
  return on that investment.

- This does not happen in reality, though, and in his 1990
  article "Why Doesn't Capital Flow from Rich to Poor
  Countries?" the American economist Robert E. Lucas Jr.*
  showed very simply, over six pages, that modern economic
  theory cannot explain why.

- This, the Lucas paradox,* has become one of the central
  questions in economic development.* It has both inspired
  a great deal of research and attracted interest from the
  wider public who want to get to the root cause of why poor
  countries stay poor.

Who Is Robert E. Lucas Jr.?

The economist Robert E. Lucas Jr., author of the essay "Why Doesn't
Capital Flow from Rich to Poor Countries?" (1990), was born in the
city of Yakima in the US state of Washington[1] in 1937 and grew up in
the northwest of the United States. His parents were New Deal*
Democrats* and happy to disagree with friends and neighbors about

economics. (The New Deal was a set of domestic policies implemented by President Franklin D. Roosevelt* in the United States between 1933 and 1938, in response to the catastrophic economic crisis known as the Great Depression;* these policies included large amounts of government spending intended to speed America's economic recovery. "Democrats" refers to the largest center-left party in the United States.) Speaking of his parents, Lucas said: "Their parents and most of our relatives and neighbors were Republicans,* [the largest right-wing party in the United States] so they were self-conscious in their liberalism and took it as emblematic of their ability to think for themselves."[2]

Although as a student he was strongest at mathematics and science, Lucas received his undergraduate degree in history from the University of Chicago in 1959. Having decided that it was actually economics that drove historical events and development, Lucas went on to study the subject, also at Chicago, obtaining his PhD in 1964.

Lucas began a career in academia and eventually returned to Chicago as an economics professor in 1974. He won the Nobel Prize in Economics* in 1995, and has been described as the most influential scholar of macroeconomics* of the last quarter of the twentieth century (that is, the branch of economics that deals with the effect of various forces on national, regional, and global economies).[3]

While studying for his PhD, Lucas attended a class taught by the renowned economist Milton Friedman;*he described it as a "life-changing experience." Friedman's approach taught Lucas two concrete lessons we can easily see in "Why Doesn't Capital Flow?" The first was a "willingness to follow ... economic logic wherever it led." The second was the ability to translate this logic into mathematics, which in turn made his reasoning more exact. "I knew I would never be able to think as fast as Friedman," he was to say, "but I also knew that if I developed a reliable, systematic way for approaching economic problems I would end up at the right place."

What Does "Why Doesn't Capital Flow from Rich to Poor Countries?" Say?

In his 1990 article "Why Doesn't Capital Flow?" Lucas writes that twentieth-century modern economic theory predicts that "investment goods [or capital goods, which are used to produce other goods and include machinery, buildings, and tools] would flow rapidly from the United States and other wealthy countries to India and other poor countries. Indeed, one would expect no investment to occur in the wealthy countries …"[4] Capital is scarcer in poor countries than in rich ones so it should stand to reason that investors will earn more by investing their money where capital is rarer than where it is more plentiful. Indeed, they should see poor countries as profitable places to invest in—so much so, in fact, that all investment should go there until the amount of capital relative to labor* (that is, the human effort used in production) becomes the same in both rich and poor countries.

Lucas's article notes that these assumptions are "drastically wrong," asking "exactly what is wrong with them, and what assumptions should replace them?" The argument he makes has since been called the Lucas paradox.

Lucas explores several possible explanations for the paradox. He considers the effects of human capital*—the education, knowledge and skills of people. He also looks at various forms of market failure*— situations where markets fail to allocate goods and services efficiently because of factors such as imperfect information (where one party in a transaction is better informed than the other), or a fear that a borrowing country will not enforce contracts.

While Lucas did not invent these ideas of human capital or imperfect institutions, he did think about them in new, systematic ways. In the process he showed that mainstream economics makes predictions that do not make sense based on what we actually see in the world.

Consider the fact, for instance, that capital does not flow as freely as modern economic theory predicted from developed wealthy nations to poorer developing nations. According to this theory, there should be no motive for labor to flow the other way. But, warns Lucas, "we do not want to resolve the puzzle of capital flows [the movement of money] with a theory that predicts, contrary to the evidence provided by millions of Mexicans, that Mexican workers can earn equal wages in the United States and in Mexico."

Lucas's description of this paradox struck a chord with both economists and members of the public. In his view, the failure of modern economics to explain the paradox is not just of theoretical* interest; it also poses a "central question for economic development."

Lucas's research has inspired many other scholars to look into flows of capital between rich and poor nations. His short, concise article almost single-handedly opened up the topic to anyone interested in economics or poverty.

Why Does "Why Doesn't Capital Flow from Rich to Poor Countries?" Matter?

It is hard to overstate the influence of the Lucas paradox. It has driven many scholars to look for explanations in the fundamentals of developing economies, and in the imperfections of the global capital markets that might explain why theory does not offer accurate predictions.

"Why Doesn't Capital Flow?" points out the flaws in predictions of neoclassical economics*—a modern approach that builds on the tradition of classical economics.* To define these approaches more specifically:

- Classical economics dates back to the Scottish philosopher Adam Smith,* who in 1776 published the book *The Wealth of Nations* in which he argues that society is best served by a free market where people compete economically as they see fit, with limited government interference. Under such a system the "invisible hand" of the market would keep prices low, encourage innovation, and see capital allocated where it is needed most.

Neoclassical economics refines these ideas in a number of mathematically driven ways. It introduces the concept of marginal returns:* the change in output (that is, the goods or services produced in a specific time period by a company, industry, or state) from the last unit of input (that is, the resources used to produce output). Marginal returns might be gained, for example, by hiring a sixth worker for a team of five on an assembly line. According to neoclassical economics, labor and capital will seek out higher marginal returns until an equilibrium*—a stable state when supply and demand are balanced—is reached. It holds that people will make rational* economic decisions based on their own self-interest, considering both economic and noneconomic factors.

The neoclassical approach is the current basis for the entire world economy, and for the reforms in poorer countries that the international community encourages.

Lucas is one of the most important figures in the Chicago school,* an influential group of economists who are champions of the free market. The Chicago school recommends deregulation* (less government interference in the economic system). It is opposed to a competing Keynesian* approach (named after the famous British economist John Maynard Keynes*), according to which governments should play a bigger role in economics, and should borrow money to stimulate the economy during recessions. The Chicago school has been dominant since the 1970s, largely because of the work of Lucas and his fellow American economist Milton Friedman. Since the 2008 financial crisis,* however, there has been increased support for the Keynesian view.

"Why Doesn't Capital Flow?" also reveals some fundamental issues about modern economics scholarship. Economics uses ambitious, simplified generalizations, often expressed with mathematics, to explain complex features of the real world. When these generalizations lead to predictions that do not hold true in real life, economists tend to do more research and look at other variables to introduce into their economic models. They often resist the idea that the models might just be wrong.

Two and a half decades after its publication, "Why Doesn't Capital Flow?" is still vital reading for anyone interested in the gap between rich and poor countries, and why poor countries have remained poor.

NOTES

1   Tore Frängsmyr, ed., *Les Prix Nobel: The Nobel Prizes 1995* (Stockholm: Nobel Foundation, 1996).

2   Robert E. Lucas Jr. in Frängsmyr, *Les Prix Nobel*.

3   N. Gregory Mankiw, "Back in Demand," *Wall Street Journal* (September 21, 2009), http://www.wsj.com/articles/SB10001424052970204518504574417810281734756.

4   Robert E. Lucas Jr., "Why Doesn't Capital Flow from Rich to Poor Countries?," *American Economic Review* 80 (1990): 92–6.

SECTION 1
INFLUENCES

THE AUTHOR AND THE HISTORICAL CONTEXT

KEY POINTS

- Robert E. Lucas Jr.'s childhood exposed him to the principle that mathematics might be applied to practical problems, and to the role of capital* in the success or failure of small businesses such as his parents' restaurant in Seattle.

- "Why Doesn't Capital Flow?" began a new way of investigating poverty and international investment.

- Lucas wrote the article at a time when powerful global leaders were actively supporting the expansion of free markets.

Why Read This Text?

Robert E. Lucas Jr.'s groundbreaking article "Why Doesn't Capital Flow from Rich to Poor Countries?" (1990) deals with questions concerning neoclassical economics.* According to neoclassical theory, capital (money) should continually move toward the world's poorer countries because of the potential for higher returns there. The international market should naturally seek equilibrium*—a stable state when supply and demand are balanced—through the most efficient allocation of resources, and through forces such as pricing.

But in the real world, contrary to neoclassical economics, capital does not flow to the poorer developing nations where it is needed most. Lucas's article addresses this fact.

Lucas's work focuses on the importance of human skill and experience in supporting economic development,* and on international market failures* (situations where goods and services are

> ❝ "In the fall of 1960, I began Milton Friedman's price theory sequence. I had been looking forward to this famous course all summer, but it was far more exciting than anything I had imagined. What made it so? Many Chicago students have tried to answer this question. Certainly Friedman's brilliance and intensity, and his willingness to follow his economic logic wherever it led all played a role. ❞
>
> Robert E. Lucas Jr., biography, www.nobelprize.org

not allocated efficiently by market forces). According to him, "the egalitarian*predictions of the simplest neoclassical models of trade and growth are well known and easy to explain."[1] In simple terms, the "egalitarian" principle means that, if capital markets are free and competitive, new investment should mainly occur only in poorer countries, because returns on this investment would be greater there.

"Why Doesn't Capital Flow?" became the foundation for a new discipline of neoclassical development economics, which has gained worldwide importance. A number of scholars since have tried to offer ways of understanding persistently low capital investment in the developing world, while staying within the assumptions of neoclassical economics.

Author's Life

Lucas is the child of a small-business owner father and a mother who worked in the field of fashion as an artist; both backed the New Deal*—a suite of economic policies implemented by President Franklin D. Roosevelt* in response to the economic crisis known as the Great Depression.* While they were supporters of the largest center-left party in the US, the Democratic Party,* their social and family environment was mainly Republican* (America's largest right-wing party). After his parents' first business, an ice-cream restaurant,

17

failed during the Great Depression, Lucas's father taught himself enough mathematics and engineering to become president of a refrigeration company. Speaking of his father, Lucas said, "When I took calculus in high school, he enlisted my help on a refrigeration design problem he was working on—and actually used my calculations! It was my first taste of real applied mathematics, and an exciting one." Applying mathematics to understanding real world problems clearly had a lasting effect on Lucas. Using mathematics to see predictions that logically flow from assumptions is a central theme of "Why Doesn't Capital Flow?"

Lucas received his undergraduate degree in history from the University of Chicago, where he would complete his doctorate in economics. His time as a student of economists such as Milton Friedman* left him solidly grounded within the neoclassical school of economics, which emphasizes mathematical rigor and approaches both individual (or microeconomic*) economic behavior, and national and global level (or macroeconomic*) economic patterns, according to the same methods and assumptions.

Lucas wrote "Why Doesn't Capital Flow?" as a professor at the University of Chicago, where he has taught since 1974. His work earned him a Nobel Prize in Economics* five years later.

Author's Background

Throughout "Why Doesn't Capital Flow?" Lucas compares the United States and India, and observes that if the assumptions of neoclassical economics are true, the marginal returns*(the additional output resulting from a change of input) from investment in India should be about 58 times higher than they are in America.

Lucas wrote his article at a time when Western governments were strongly committed to free-market policies: economic policies in which the market is allowed to operate without governmental regulation or interference. When Lucas published the article in 1990, the Republican Ronald Reagan* had recently completed eight years as president of the United States, and the Conservative* Margaret Thatcher* was ending eleven years as prime minister in the United Kingdom. Like the American Republican Party, the British Conservative Party is an economically and socially right-wing party; both parties had fiercely promoted private enterprise as the most important part of democratic* economies, passing laws and government policies that helped deregulate* the financial industry and curb the actions of industrial unions* and collective bargaining* (negotiations between employers and employees over issues such as wages and working conditions).

These policies also affected debates over development in the developing world. Beginning in the 1950s, the mainstream theory of development suggested that import tariffs* (taxes to make imported goods more expensive than domestically produced goods) and other barriers to free trade were the best way to bring about rapid development in poorer countries. Such measures were thought to help developing countries promote their own goods and strengthen their economies. During the 1980s and 1990s, however, the neoclassical economics at the center of Reaganite and Thatcherite policies held that a free market was the best way to bring about rapid development in the developing world. As a result, when Lucas was writing, the free flow of capital and goods, though not of people, was very much in vogue, keeping with the view of mainstream economics that free-market policies would lead to greater growth.

NOTES

1   Robert E. Lucas Jr., "Why Doesn't Capital Flow from Rich to Poor Countries?," *American Economic Review* 80 (1990): 92.

MODULE 2
ACADEMIC CONTEXT

KEY POINTS

- The economic development* of poorer nations—the process of achieving prosperity and raising living standards—has always been of great interest in the discipline of economics.

- Capital*—that is, money that may be invested—has played a leading role in development theories. These ranged from mercantilism* in the seventeenth century (which measured a state's prosperity based on the amount of capital it held in gold and silver bullion*), to the 1960 linear stages-of-growth* theory, which assumed that development would take a similar path in every country.

- The stages-of-growth theory was criticized for not sufficiently considering aspects of development other than capital.

The Work in its Context

Robert E. Lucas Jr.'s article "Why Doesn't Capital Flow from Rich to Poor Countries?" is useful to scholars of development economics (the study of matters concerning prosperity in poor countries).

Study in this field begins with mercantilist ideas that appeared in the seventeenth century. Mercantilists believed that growing wealthier was a question of maximizing exports while minimizing imports; they tried to achieve this by imposing tariffs* (taxes on imports) and by providing subsidies* (financial help from government) to their own industries. A positive balance of trade* was deemed most important, meaning that exports should exceed imports. Many of these ideas continued into the nineteenth century.

Development economics as a field grew quickly in the years after

> ❝ The central idea of virtually all postwar development policies is to stimulate transfers of capital goods from rich to poor countries. ❞
>
> Robert E. Lucas Jr., "Why Doesn't Capital Flow from Rich to Poor Countries?"

World War II,* spurred by the long period of grave tension between the United States and the Soviet Union* known as the Cold War,* and by many former European colonies claiming their independence. An important early theory was the "stages-of-growth" approach developed in the 1950s by American economist W. W. Rostow* which saw development as a linear, broadly similar process from country to country. This theory lay behind the foreign-aid policies of Presidents John F. Kennedy* and Lyndon B. Johnson* in the 1960s. Critics said Rostow's stages-of-growth approach did not adequately consider differences between countries, or aspects of development other than capital.

Dependency theory*, an approach formed in the 1950s in academic papers by the British economist Hans Singer* and the Argentinian economist Raúl Prebisch,* became popular in the 1960s and 1970s. According to the theory, developed countries (called the "center") controlled innovation in technology, and used the developing world (the "periphery") for inexpensive raw materials and labor and as markets for finished goods. Singer and Prebisch recommended that developing countries should impose tariffs and barriers to trade in an effort to substitute their own goods for those imported from the developed world. This was called import-substitution industrialization,* and it was particularly popular in Latin America.

Dependency theory fell out of favor in the 1980s and 1990s in both university departments and in world capitals, where economic policies were implemented. Neoclassical* principles held that tariffs and other barriers to trade should be removed, and that an unobstructed free market was the best way to bring about rapid development in the developing world.

Overview of the Field

In 1990, Lucas's "Why Doesn't Capital Flow?" drew on many of the core concepts of neoclassical economics:

- Investors are rational,* fully informed, and pursue their own self-interests in both economic and noneconomic ways (economists call this maximized utility:* a rational actor will make decisions that will maximize their happiness or well-being)

- Return on investment will be higher where there is less capital per worker because of the law of diminishing returns,* meaning that there is a point after which an additional unit of capital or labor will produce less of a return than the unit before it (that is, the point where further investment in labor or money is not useful)

- Return on investment will be higher where there is less capital per worker because of the law of diminishing returns,* meaning that there is a point after which an additional unit of capital or labor will produce less of a return than the unit before it (that is, the point where further investment in labor or money is not useful)

- Markets are efficient, and will reflect all information correctly in prices.

The Lucas paradox* arose from the fact that only about 10 per cent of cross-border capital flow goes to poor countries.[1] Poor countries have increased the share of this capital they attract, but at the same time, rich countries are themselves major recipients of capital from developing countries. So not only does capital not mostly flow from rich countries to poorer countries, but those with capital in poorer countries prefer to invest it in wealthier countries—the conspicuous opposite of what economic theory would predict.

Lucas also identifies a second aspect of the paradox, which is that the capital of developed nations that is invested in the developing world tends to go to the developing countries that are wealthier and more advanced. Neoclassical economic theory, however, predicts that capital will go to the poorest countries that have the lowest amounts of capital per worker.

Academic Influences

Lucas attempts to approach the issues of development and world poverty within the framework of the Chicago school* tradition. He represents the third generation of these economists, who are associated with the University of Chicago. The first generation, represented in the mid-twentieth century by Frank Knight,* an economist whose work concerned risk and uncertainty, held that while the free market may be inefficient, government intervention is even less efficient. The economist Milton Friedman* was a leading member of the second generation. His work on the supply of money—the amount of money available to an economy at any time—led him to view a stable (and slightly increasing) supply of money as the most important predictor of economic growth—an approach known as monetarism.* He was the most visible enthusiast of the free market as the engine of growth for poorer countries.

Lucas was a student of Friedman's, and belongs to the third generation. He shares Friedman's view that monetary instability adds to the problem of poverty, but believes that underlying instabilities are probably not caused by the supply of money or rate of inflation. (More generally, the emphasis of the Chicago school shifts in the third generation from monetarism to work revolving around rational expectations,* a field of research that investigates how people make best guesses about the future by using all available information. This is the work for which Lucas received his Nobel Prize.) Lucas also agrees with the economist W. W. Rostow (who created the linear approach to understanding development) that economic growth is "always associated with a movement out of agriculture and into the city environment."[2]

NOTES

1   Moritz Schularick, "A Tale of Two 'Globalizations': Capital Flows from Rich to Poor in Two Eras of Global Finance," *International Journal of Finance and Economics* 11 (2006): 339–54, doi:10.1002/ijfe.302.

2   EconTalk episode with Bob Lucas, hosted by Russ Roberts, "Lucas on Growth, Poverty, and Business Cycles," *Library of Economics and Liberty* (February 5, 2007), http://www.econtalk.org/archives/2007/02/lucas_on_ growth.html.

MODULE 3
THE PROBLEM

KEY POINTS

- Lucas's text launches two principal inquiries: "The assumptions [made by mainstream economics] on technology and trade flow must be drastically wrong, but what exactly is wrong with them, and what assumptions should replace them?"[1]

- At the time when Lucas was writing, most people in the Chicago school* argued that free markets, left to their own devices with a minimum of government intervention, would best lead to economic growth in the world's poorer countries. Government action would be more likely to introduce inefficiencies and bad incentives.

- Lucas, who largely built upon the arguments and assumptions of the mainstream debate, was the first to show that it could not explain the actual way in which capital* flows to the developing world.

Core Question

In "Why Doesn't Capital Flow from Rich to Poor Countries?" Robert E. Lucas Jr. compares the United States and India, and methodically takes the reader through a complex series of mathematical calculations. He observes that if assumptions made by neoclassical economics are true, the marginal product* of capital (that is, the return on investment) in India ought—at the time he was writing—to be about 58 times what it is in America.[2] The marginal product means the effect of the *next* unit—so the next dollar of investment should accomplish 58 times as much if you sent it to Bangalore than if you sent it to Boston.

> ❝ Then the law of diminishing returns implies that the marginal product of capital is higher in the less productive (i.e. in the poorer) economy. If so, then if trade in capital good is free and competitive, new investment will occur only in the poorer economy, and this will continue to be true until capital-labor ratios, and hence wages and capital returns, are equalized. ❞
>
> Robert E. Lucas Jr., "Why Doesn't Capital Flow from Rich to Poor Countries?"

If this model is anywhere close to being accurate, and if world capital markets are largely free of national barriers, then investment should flow rapidly from the United States and other rich countries to India and other developing countries. "Indeed," Lucas argues, "one would expect *no* investment to occur in the wealthy countries in the face of return differentials of this magnitude."[3]

The prediction of modern economics theory is that all capital will flow to where returns should be highest, until the capital invested per worker is the same everywhere—a state that economists call "equilibrium."* Lucas notes that this prediction is "drastically wrong" in the actual world.

The Participants

In the years after World War II,* economic models measured growth chiefly through physical capital—tangible assets such as equipment, for example. The most sophisticated of these models was the Solow model* produced by the Nobel Prize*-winning economist Robert Solow* in 1956.[4] In this model, the law of diminishing returns* suggests countries will eventually come together on the same path of growth—countries with less capital per person would grow faster, and wealthier nations would grow more slowly, until they all end up with the same ratio of capital to labor* and an identical rate of growth.

Eventually they would reach an equilibrium, after which their exact growth rate would depend on the sophistication of their technology and population size.[5]

Lucas rejects these models because they do not explain the difference in growth that actually takes place, with the richest countries having 25 times the income per person of the poorest. And instead of having technology and population treated as given (as "exogenous factors"*—variables that come from outside an economic model), Lucas prefers to explain both within his model. The name for this approach is an "endogenous growth theory":* a model that treats economic growth as the result of investment in innovation and knowledge, rather than as an exogenous (unexplained) variable such as the rate of technological progress.

For Lucas, human capital* can be measured by the market value of a person acquiring additional skills or qualifications. The additional pay they will receive for having undertaken a university degree or other form of training is a measure of that added human capital's worth. And crucially, unlike with physical capital, the law of diminishing returns does *not* apply to human capital. It produces spillover effects: people learn from each other. As Lucas describes it, "human-capital accumulation is a fundamentally *social* activity, involving *groups* of people in a way that has no counterpart in the accumulation of physical capital."[6] Based on another set of methodical calculations, he concludes that "a 10 percent increase in the average quality of those with whom I work [that is, their human capital] increases my productivity by 3.6 percent."[7]

Though this all seems quite cheery, there is a negative element. The diminishing returns of physical capital were precisely why Solow's model predicts the growth rates of rich and poor countries would come together over time. By factoring in human capital Lucas's endogenous growth model sought to explain why rich and poor nations might have different growth rates over quite long periods of time, as richer countries have higher levels of human capital to begin with.

The Contemporary Debate

When Lucas wrote "Why Doesn't Capital Flow?" economists generally agreed that human capital was an important aspect of growth. The American economist Kenneth Arrow* suggested in 1962 that formal education and on-the-job training enhance an individual's skills, thereby increasing productivity.[8] Other researchers in 1966 said education is more likely to encourage workers to use new processes and technologies effectively.[9] Lucas himself had argued, two years before, that education increased a country's growth by boosting its capacity for innovation.[10]

Occasionally, researchers would question whether widespread education could meet all these hopes for a nation's development. One group of three researchers in 1991 looked at 58 countries, and found education had positive effects on growth in East Asia, insignificant effects in South Asia and Latin America, and, curiously, apparently negative effects in Africa and the Middle East.[11]

While Lucas shares the approach of his Chicago school predecessors Gary Becker* and Jacob Mincer* in how he treats human capital, he departs from them by broadening the application of the concept to overseas development and, in particular, investment. Previous analyses tended to focus on human capital only within America. In "Why Doesn't Capital Flow?" Lucas's bigger-picture analysis of the relationship between international investment capital and human capital represented a fresh research approach.

NOTES

1   Robert E. Lucas Jr., "Why Doesn't Capital Flow from Rich to Poor
     Countries?," *American Economic Review* 80 (1990): 92.

2   Lucas, "Why Doesn't Capital Flow," 92, cites Robert Summers and Alan
     Heston, "A New Set of International Comparisons of Real Product and Price
     Levels: Estimates for 130 Countries, 1950–85," *Review of Income and
     Wealth* 34, no. 1 (March 1988): 1–25, doi:10.1111/j.1475-4991.1988.
     tb00558.x.

3   Lucas, "Why Doesn't Capital Flow," 92.

4   Robert M. Solow, "A Contribution to the Theory of Economic Growth,"
     Quarterly Journal of Economics 70, no. 1 (February 1956): 65–94, http://
     www.jstor.org/stable/1884513?origin=JSTOR-pdf&seq=1#page_scan_tab_
     contents.

5   Robert Skidelsky, "The Mystery of Growth," *New York Review of Books*
     (March 13, 2003), http://www.nybooks.com/articles/2003/03/13/the-
     mystery-of-growth/.

6   Robert E. Lucas Jr., "On the Mechanics of Economic Development," *Journal
     of Monetary Economics* 22, no. 1 (1988): 3–42.

7   Lucas, "Why Doesn't Capital Flow," 94.

8   Kenneth J. Arrow, "The Economic Implications of Learning by Doing," *Review
     of Economic Studies* 29, no. 3 (June 1962): 155–73, http://www.jstor.org/
     stable/2295952?seq=1#page_scan_tab_contents.

9   Richard R. Nelson and Edmund S. Phelps, "Investment in Humans,
     Technology Diffusion, and Economic Growth," *American Economic Review*
     56, no. 2 (1966), 69–75.

10   Lucas, "On the Mechanics of Economic Development."

11   Lawrence J. Lau et al., "Education and Productivity in Developing Countries:
     An Aggregate Production Function Approach," World Bank policy research
     working paper WPS612 (March 31, 1991).

THE AUTHOR'S CONTRIBUTION

KEY POINTS

- Robert E. Lucas Jr.'s primary aim in "Why Doesn't Capital Flow?" is to explore the question in his title. He wants to spark debate and incite research to enable neoclassical economists* to better understand poverty in developing nations.

- The author's simple but original argument about the persistently low level of international capital* investment from rich countries in developing nations*—and the mathematical proof behind this argument—broke new ground in the field of development* economics (the study of economic matters concerning development).

- India launched free-market reforms the year after "Why Doesn't Capital Flow?" was published, and has become the world's fastest-growing economy just 25 years after serving as Lucas's primary example of a poor country.

Author's Aims

Before publishing "Why Doesn't Capital Flow from Rich to Poor Countries?" in 1990, Lucas gave a series of lectures in 1984 and 1985 at the University of Cambridge in England with the title "On the Mechanics of Economic Development." The lectures introduced his dissatisfaction with traditional theories of economic growth, and his search for an alternative. He started with assumptions about rationality* in human behavior (that is, the capacity of human beings to act on decisions made after considering all the information available), and used the assumptions to explain the patterns of economic growth and development we actually observe in the world.

> 66 The diversity across countries in measured per capita income levels is literally too great to be believed. Compared to the 1980 average for what the World Bank calls the 'industrial market economies' (Ireland up through Switzerland) of US $10,000, India's per capita income is $240, Haiti's is $270, and so on for the rest of the very poorest countries. This is a difference of a factor of 40 in living standards! These latter figures are too low to sustain life in, say, England or the United States … 99
> Robert E. Lucas Jr., "On the Mechanics of Economic Development"

He developed these themes further in the article "Why Doesn't Capital Flow?" by focusing on marginal returns*—the effect of adding the last unit of capital, as opposed to focusing on the total amount of capital.

The law of diminishing returns* indicates that the marginal returns from invested capital should be lower where there is already more capital invested per worker—that is, in richer countries—and higher where there is less, in developing countries. Therefore, if capital markets are free and competitive, then rational investors should invest only in poorer countries until wages, returns on investment, and capital-labor ratios (the amount of capital required for a certain amount of labor* to be performed) are equal across all countries.

Lucas demonstrates mathematically that this does not happen in the real world, and then examines four possible causes for this state of affairs, now known as the Lucas paradox.* He also discusses what donor countries can do to improve the likelihood of developing countries receiving investment.

Approach

In his approach, Lucas very much sticks to the concerns and methods of the Chicago school* and neoclassical economics.*

Like members of the Chicago school since the economist Frank Knight,* Lucas focuses heavily on theory. He assumes the rationality of the people he studies, and starts with certain assumptions about their goals and preferences. He then uses mathematics to make predictions based on movement toward equilibrium* (when supply and demand are perfectly balanced).

To an extent, Lucas's inquiries about capital and the developing world resemble his earlier work on rational expectations,* for which he later won the Nobel Prize.*[1] He talks about actors (investors), assumptions about their goals (maximized returns), and the way they will go about pursuing these (rationality).

"Why Doesn't Capital Flow?" also resembles Lucas's early work about how questions of macroeconomics* (economic behavior at the national and international level) relate to microeconomics*[2] (economic behavior at the level of the individual). It is also like both earlier works in his heavy use of mathematics; here, however, he focuses on understanding questions of economic development in the developing world.

Contribution in Context

Lucas was not the first economist to apply the assumptions of the Chicago school to the questions of development in poorer countries. The influential economist Milton Friedman* encouraged free-market reforms as the swiftest way of raising a country out of poverty, and pointed to Hong Kong, Estonia, and Iceland as case studies.[3] In Friedman's view, international investors would be attracted by countries pursuing policies of deregulation.*

The approach of Chicago school thinkers like Friedman is to trust markets to raise living standards in the developing world. While Lucas is very much in that school, he also demonstrates how the very same assumptions behind that view predict something that is not the case in reality—that market forces should send investment to the poorest countries.

The concepts of diminishing returns* and maximizing utility,* being central to an economist's theoretical* toolkit, did not originate with Lucas. The novelty in his work lies in his comprehensive demonstration, using mathematics, that these concepts produced a paradox—subsequently called the Lucas paradox.

Lucas often uses India as an example. Whether by coincidence or not, the year after the 1990 publication of "Why Doesn't Capital Flow?," Prime Minister Narasimha Rao* instigated a round of free-market reforms in India that led to rapidly increased growth. In 2015, India was the fastest-growing economy in the world.

NOTES

1   Robert E. Lucas Jr., "Expectations and the Neutrality of Money," *Journal of Economic Theory* 4, no. 2 (April 1972): 103–24.

2   Robert E. Lucas Jr., "Econometric Policy Evaluation: A Critique," in *The Phillips Curve and Labor Markets* by Karl Brunner and Allan Meltzer, Carnegie-Rochester Conference Series on Public Policy (New York: American Elsevier, 1976): 19–46.

3   Milton Friedman, "The Real Lesson of Hong Kong," *National Review* (December 31, 1997).

SECTION 2
IDEAS

MAIN IDEAS

KEY POINTS

- Lucas discusses two key points: the difference in human capital* between the developed and the developing world, and the effects of human capital on surrounding workers.

- He also explores three other areas—political risk* (the possibility that an investment or loan could suffer because of political instability or government decisions) and market failures* (situations where markets fail to allocate goods and services efficiently); monopolies* (when a supplier controls the supply of a commodity or service and can set its price higher than would otherwise be possible) and colonial* powers; and whether there is prejudice in developing countries against foreign investors and their capital.*

- Each of these might provide an answer to the paradox* Lucas identifies in his title.

Key Themes

In "Why Doesn't Capital Flow from Rich to Poor Countries?" Robert E. Lucas Jr. argues that it is important to know which is more correct out of the possible suggestions he offers to his question (two having to do with human capital, one with imperfections in capital markets, and one with monopolistic investors), as they imply very different courses of action for foreign aid policy. In many cases, he notes, the benefit of government foreign aid will be offset by a reduction in the amount of private investment a country receives from overseas, or will result in an increase in private investment in other countries from that country.

Lucas discusses human capital—the skills or knowledge that the

> ❝ The assumptions ... must be drastically wrong, but what exactly is wrong with them, and what assumptions should replace them? This is a central question for economic development. I consider four candidate answers to this question. ❞
>
> Robert E. Lucas Jr., "Why Doesn't Capital Flow from Rich to Poor Countries?"

people in a nation or a company possess—as one possible reason why capital doesn't flow from rich to poor countries. Since there are different levels of education in the developed world than there are in rich nations, Lucas finds that—at the time he wrote—the average worker in the United States or Canada had roughly five times the human capital of an average worker in India or Ghana. An average American worker in 1987 earned about $24,000 in a year; by Lucas's calculations, an average worker from India or Ghana would earn $4,800 that year working in America.[1]

Lucas does not want to forget about the effects of human capital on surrounding workers either. After some calculations based on the analysis of previous research, Lucas suggests that a 10 percent increase in the average quality [that is, their human capital—their level of education, technical training, and skills acquired on the job] of the people around you will increase your productivity by 3.6 per cent.[2]

Lucas thinks the combination of differences in human capital between richer and poorer countries and the infectious effects of human capital may be enough in itself to explain why capital does not flow from rich countries to poor countries. But this requires the assumption that human capital will only affect people in geographical proximity—not those in other countries.

Lucas goes on to consider other possibilities: whether political risk in the developing world might be deterring investors from richer countries; whether the legacies of monopoly or colonialism might also be playing a role; and whether developing countries might be prejudiced against foreign investors.

Exploring the Ideas

Lucas has been praised for demonstrating his key ideas in "Why Doesn't Capital Flow?" with very rigorous mathematics, though you don't actually have to understand how the math works to understand his general ideas. A key concept here is the Cobb-Douglas production function,* which examines the relationship between capital and labor.*[3] It was named for the economists Charles Cobb* and Paul Douglas,* who developed and tested it between 1927 and 1947. This sophisticated equation shows how capital and labor come together to create production (in this context, the value of goods made in a year). It relates production (y), capital (x), productivity (A) and a constant (a technological element that stays the same—β), in the following way:

$$y = Ax^\beta$$

… with y representing the income per worker, and x the capital per worker. So for the mathematically minded among you, you're differentiating dy/dx (i.e. the change in y, per unit of change in x) that corresponds to the marginal effect of capital (dy/dx, represented as r), and can be written as:

$$r = A\,\beta x^{\beta-1}$$

or, substituting y for x:

$$r = \beta A^{1/\beta} y^{(\beta-1)/\beta}$$

While it is not necessary to be able to analyze this calculation for the purpose of understanding Lucas's text, if you are mathematically inclined you might be interested to note that Lucas does this by solving for x (x meaning capital input: the value of all machinery, buildings and equipment), using the average value of β for the United States and India, and then differentiating.

If you don't particularly enjoy mathematics, all you need to know is that with this equation Lucas is representing the marginal product of capital (meaning the additional output resulting from an input of physical capital—like equipment or buildings).

Using an equation like this and taking from other research the finding that production (y) in the United States is about 15 times what it is in India,[4] Lucas finds that the marginal return* of capital (x) in India (the change in output from the last unit of input in Indian industry) *should* be 58 times what it is in the United States.[5] This is the basis of his argument that investment capital *should* flow, quickly, to India and other developing countries.

Language and Expression

Lucas's style has been described as having a great deal of "mathiness."[6] In his time as a student at the University of Chicago, he writes, he would attempt to go home and work out in mathematics the verbal arguments that Milton Friedman* made in his price theory* class ("price theory" refers to inquiry into the ways prices are set by the interaction of supply and demand). He says, "After every class, I tried to translate what Friedman had done into the mathematics I had learned from [Paul] Samuelson.* I knew I would never be able to think as fast as Friedman, but I also knew that if I developed a reliable, systematic way for approaching economic problems I would end up at the right place."[7] (Paul Samuelson was the author of *Foundations of Economic Analysis*, which Lucas had read during his first summer as a University of Chicago postgraduate.)[8]

The result of this training early in his career has given Lucas his distinctive sharp eye when analyzing particular assumptions (the prediction that capital will flow from rich countries to poor ones, for example). By simplifying the assumptions and using rigorous mathematics to describe relationships, he can find unusual or paradoxical implications.

This approach, however, makes much of his work inaccessible to people without advanced training in economics and mathematics. It becomes even less accessible because, in addition to the sophisticated mathematics, Lucas also explains his goals and assumptions in complex ways. For instance, he described his work in making economic models as imagining "a mechanical, artificial world, populated by ... interacting robots ... that is capable of exhibiting behavior the gross features of which resemble those of the actual world ..."[9]

While the British economic historian Robert Skidelsky* notes, somewhat dryly, that "this is not a sales pitch for a wide readership," he notes also that even the nonspecialist reader can come to feel some of the excitement of Lucas's passionate search for the mystery underlying economic growth.[10]

NOTES

1   Robert E. Lucas Jr., "Why Doesn't Capital Flow from Rich to Poor Countries?," *American Economic Review* 80 (1990): 93.

2   Lucas "Why Doesn't Capital Flow," 94.

3   Charles W. Cobb and Paul H. Douglas, "A Theory of Production," *American Economic Review* 18, no. 1, supplement (March 1928): 139–65, http://www2.econ.iastate.edu/classes/econ521/orazem/Papers/cobb-douglas.pdf.

4   Robert Summers and Alan Heston, "A New Set of International Comparisons of Real Product and Price Levels: Estimates for 130 Countries, 1950–85," *Review of Income and* Wealth, 34, no. 1 (March 1988), pp. 18–21, doi:10.1111/j.1475-4991.1988.tb00558.x.

5   Lucas, "Why Doesn't Capital Flow," 92.

6   Paul M. Romer [Lucas was Romer's doctoral supervisor], "Mathiness in the Theory of Economic Growth," *American Economic Review* 105, no. 5 (2015): 89–93, https://www.aeaweb.org/articles.php?doi=10.1257/aer.p20151066.

7   Robert E. Lucas Jr. in Tore Frängsmy, ed., *Les Prix Nobel: The Nobel Prizes 1995* (Stockholm: Nobel Foundation, 1996).

8   Paul A. Samuelson, *Foundations of Economic Analysis* (Cambridge: Harvard University Press, 1983).

9   Robert E. Lucas Jr., "On the Mechanics of Economic Development," *Journal of Monetary Economics* 22 (1988): 3–42, http://www.parisschoolofeconomics.eu/docs/darcillon-thibault/lucasmechanicseconomicgrowth.pdf.

10 Robert Skidelsky, "The Mystery of Growth," *New York Review of Books* (March 13, 2003).

MODULE 6
SECONDARY IDEAS

KEY POINTS

- One of the main secondary ideas in "Why Doesn't Capital Flow?" is political risk*—the possibility that an investment or loan could suffer because of a nation's political instability or government policy. For Lucas, however, this is not an adequate explanation as to why capital* does not fly from rich to poor countries.

- Other ideas Lucas mentions include whether monopolies* (the situation that arises when a trader is able to set a price for a good or service very high because it is the only supplier) or colonial* powers would slow down capital transfer, and if developing countries might be prejudiced against foreign investors and their capital.

- Lucas also briefly wonders whether it might help the development of poorer countries if monetary aid were tied to the liberalization of the recipients' foreign investment policies—that is, if regulations regarding foreign investment were reduced.

- His other policy implication is that developing human capital* (skills and knowledge) is essential for progress in developing countries.

Other Ideas

An important secondary idea in Robert E. Lucas Jr.'s "Why Doesn't Capital Flow from Rich to Poor Countries?" is political risk. As Lucas explains, there is not always an effective mechanism for enforcing international borrowing agreements. The lack of a reliable enforcement agent is a key market failure.*Concerns about political risk will inhibit

> 66 … [T]here must be an effective mechanism for
> enforcing international borrowing agreements.
> Otherwise, country *B* will gain by terminating its
> relationship with *A* at the point where the repayment
> period begins, and foreseeing this, country *A* will never
> lend in the first place. 99
>
> Robert E. Lucas Jr., "Why Doesn't Capital Flow from Rich to Poor Countries?"

lenders from lending, foreseeing that borrowing nations may default on their loans.

Lucas considers this explanation unsatisfactory because, he says, political risk only characterizes the relationship between rich and poor nations in the period following World War II, when developing nations claimed their independence from the European colonial* powers such as Britain and France. Before that, he argues, "a European lending to a borrower in India or the Dutch East Indies could expect his contract to be enforced with exactly the same effectiveness and by exactly the same means as a contract with a domestic borrower."[1]

Lucas argues that if this political risk only existed after 1945, rich nations' capital should have rushed to poorer parts of the world before that. Since it did not, political risk is not the main reason why capital does not flow from rich to poor countries.

He next considers whether developing countries simply do not want investment from developed nations. He describes how "otherwise attractive" poor countries such as Indonesia, the Philippines, and Iran (before the revolution of 1979 after which the nation was declared an Islamic republic), placed heavy taxes on the capita (that is, for each person) invested in their countries. He says taxes of this sort "are often explained as arising from a mistrust of foreigners or a reluctance to let developments proceed too fast." Lucas is quite cutting in dismissing this argument: referring to the pioneering

Scottish economist Adam Smith,* he says merely, "I think such explanations warrant a Smithian skepticism."[2]

Exploring the Ideas

The risk of sovereign default*—that is, the failure of a debtor country to pay back capital it had borrowed—is one example of market failure in international capital markets* (where savers lend money to countries and companies).

Another type of market failure that can be observed in international capital markets is called "moral hazard."* This occurs when one party seeks higher returns by making riskier decisions, because another party bears the risks. As interest rates rise, there is a danger that debtor nations will make riskier decisions about how to use the borrowed capital in order to increase their expected return.

There are other market failures, such as imperfect information— the borrowing country may know important details about their own economy or have plans to devalue their own currency that are unknown to the lending country.

Lucas considers political risk an unlikely explanation for the lack of capital flow from rich to poor countries; for him, political risk only arises after 1945, when the greater number of Europe's former colonies in Asia and Africa became independent. Sovereign defaults *did* take place before World War II (1939–45): Egypt under the colonial ruler Isma'il Pasha ran up debts in the 1870s that he was unable to pay after a costly war with Ethiopia. But the outcome fits with Lucas's argument, as the governments of Britain and France ultimately took control of Egypt's finance and public works ministries to see the debts repaid.

Considering the colonial period, which began to draw to a close in 1945, Lucas reflects on how, exactly, investment would be different under an imperial power (that is, a nation with a foreign empire). He argues that the imperial power can choose the level of capital invested per worker to maximize returns. After some calculations, he decides that the imperial power's "optimal policy is to retard capital flows so as to maintain real wages at artificially low levels."[3] Returning to the Cobb-Douglas production function* (the equation demonstrating the relationship between capital and labor,* and production), he calculates that the return on capital in a colony in the developing world "should be about 2.5 times the European return."[4]

Overlooked

Two arguments Lucas makes in "Why Doesn't Capital Flow?" seem both underdeveloped and overlooked. He says foreign aid should be tied to free-market reforms of the recipients' policies concerning foreign investment and that developing human capital* is essential for progress in developing countries.

The first of these is in keeping with the economic thought of the Chicago school.* The recommendations of its members such as Milton Friedman* on questions of development* (a subfield within economics aimed at raising poorer nations' standard of living) generally came down to favoring free-market reforms. The notion of conditionality* (that is, conditions set by an international financial institution that must be met if aid, a loan, or relief on its debts are to be provided to a nation) is thought-provoking, even if Lucas does not develop the idea that foreign aid should be used to reward poorer governments for lowering taxes or reducing bureaucracy.

The second policy prescription is that foreign aid should focus on developing human capital—that is, the skills and education of people in the country receiving aid. This idea is developed even less, but it is a fascinating comment as members of the Chicago school tend to be skeptical of government intervention in the economy. Here, presumably he means that education and worker training programs funded by wealthier countries would not lead to the market distortions he worries about elsewhere. Reducing human capital differentials would add further incentive for capital to flow from rich to poor countries—but Lucas is not convinced that lower levels of human capital in the latter are the only reason for low investment in developing nations.*

NOTES

1   Robert E. Lucas Jr., "Why Doesn't Capital Flow from Rich to Poor Countries?," *American Economic Review* 80 (1990), 94–5.

2   Lucas, "Why Doesn't Capital Flow," 96.

3   Lucas, "Why Doesn't Capital Flow," 95.

4   Lucas, "Why Doesn't Capital Flow," 95.

MODULE 7
ACHIEVEMENT

KEY POINTS

- Robert E. Lucas Jr.'s "Why Doesn't Capital Flow?" struck a chord both with readers interested in assumptions behind neoclassical economics* and those interested in world poverty. It also attracted the attention of policy-makers.

- Lucas received attention for a paper he published in 1988 on human capital* and endogenous growth theory* (an analysis that considers economic growth to be the result of investment in innovation and knowledge) titled "On the Mechanics of Economic Development."

- While Lucas's theoretical* findings have inspired waves of research on barriers to investment in developing countries, the main limitation of "Why Doesn't Capital Flow?" is that it does not explore how the concepts play out in the real world.

Assessing the Argument

The paradox* Robert E. Lucas Jr. identifies in "Why Doesn't Capital Flow from Rich Countries to Poor Countries?" (1990) is one of a number of major puzzles concerning the lack of flows of international capital* from rich to poor countries. He points out, for example, that a developing country's citizens do not tend to invest overseas—contrary to what we would expect from rational,* fully informed investors,[1] and asks why both investors and savers in developed countries spurn better offers overseas by borrowing and lending domestically.[2]

In each of these puzzles, fascinating questions of how they play out in the real world remain unsolved. While the concepts of human capital and political risk* were not new, Lucas's original analysis captured the interest of readers; by supporting his arguments with

> **❝** Is there some action a government of India could take that would lead the Indian economy to grow like Indonesia's or Egypt's? If so, what, exactly? ... The consequences for human welfare involved in questions like these are simply staggering: once one starts to think about them, it is hard to think about anything else. **❞**
>
> Robert E. Lucas Jr., "On the Mechanics of Economic Development"

rigorous mathematics, Lucas made his reasoning precise and persuasive, and opened up the discussion to a wide number of contributions.

Lucas introduced a new debate within the field of development* economics, based on whether the Lucas paradox* is best explained by fundamentals—government policies such as high taxes on returns (that is, distributions or payments to suppliers) or permitting high levels of inflation—or by market failures.* Capital market failures (meaning the inability to raise finance) occur when the investor has insufficient information, or when there is fear that a debtor nation will not repay its loans.

Achievement in Context

In 1988, two years before publishing "Why Doesn't Capital Flow?," Lucas wrote a celebrated paper that also revolves around the concept of human capital.

That article—"On the Mechanics of Economic Development," based on lectures he had given in England at the University of Cambridge—attracted a wide readership. This led Lucas to focus on human capital, an idea at the center of a theory of endogenous growth.

When Lucas wrote his 1988 article, economists who studied wealth and those who looked at poverty were in very different camps. Those who researched the accumulation of physical and human capital in industrial economies usually did so as macroeconomists,* focused on the economy at the level of the nation. Those who looked at poverty in the developing world were normally microeconomists,* focused on the motivations and decisions of the individual.

Lucas adapted the Solow model,* a model of economic development proposed by the economist Robert Solow* and founded on elements such as population growth, investment in machinery, and increases in productivity as a result of technological progress. In Lucas's adaptation, economic growth is driven by spillovers of human capital among people who have increased contact with each other as they move from rural areas into cities. Human capital is then, for him, the concept that can stitch together microeconomics with macroeconomics.

Not surprisingly, when Robert E. Lucas Jr. published "Why Doesn't Capital Flow?" in 1990, human capital appears again as the explanation to which he gives the most attention.

Limitations

Lucas is primarily an inventive, rigorous theoretician who has insights that are sometimes provocative and surprising. The main limitation of "Why Doesn't Capital Flow?" is its purely theoretical nature, with little examination of how the theories play out in the real world.

Lucas identifies several answers to the paradox he has identified and suggests that some of these answers seem unlikely to him. It remains for other authors to gather and measure data to determine which answer best resolves the question in his title.

The article's primarily theoretical focus shows the influence of the Chicago school* of economics; argument at the level of formal theory was typical of this approach, which may be considered a reaction to the more empirical,* evidence-based work of Keynesian* economists. Where Keynesians saw utility in government regulation, the Chicago school thought that the market would regulate itself if left to its own devices.

Chicago school approaches have also come under increasing attack since the 2008 financial crisis,* because many people—especially on the political left—thought that those approaches helped cause the crisis or made it worse.

Another issue is Lucas's narrow conception of human capital—which measures the worth of additional education and experience by their effect on a person's earnings. In fact, the idea of "human capital" was proposed in 1776 in the first work of classical* economics, *The Wealth of Nations* by the Scottish economist Adam Smith.* Smith recognizes that individual education and experience benefits society, stating, "The acquisition of such talents, by the maintenance of the acquirer during his education, study, or apprenticeship, always costs a real expense, which is a capital fixed and realized, as it were, in his person. Those talents, as they make a part of his fortune, so do they likewise that of the society to which he belongs."[3]

As an idea, human capital is then used in 1954 by the Saint Lucian economist Sir William Arthur Lewis,* who received the 1979 Nobel Prize in Economics.*[4] In neoclassical economics, the idea is first used by Gary Becker,* a University of Chicago economist and 1992 Nobel Prize winner, and author of the book *Human Capital* (1964). Becker, an undoubted influence on Lucas, presents human capital as something individuals rationally make choices about investing in, depending on expected costs and benefits. It can include both general and specific education, and habits we might choose to acquire like punctuality or sobriety.[5]

Lucas's measurement approach is limited; by focusing on changes in an individual's earnings, he does not account for any societal benefits. For example, if personal qualities like trustworthiness are part of human capital, an increase in individual trustworthiness can help support trade on a larger scale. Lucas may be neglecting an important element of human capital, but changes in earnings are more easily measurable than broader benefits.

NOTES

1 Kenneth R. French and James M. Poterba, "Investor Diversification and International Equity Markets," *American Economic Review* 81, no. 2 (1991): 222–6, http://www.nber.org/papers/w3609.

2 Martin Feldstein and Charles Horioka, "Domestic Saving and International Capital Flows," *Economic Journal* 90, no. 358 (June 1980): 314–29, http://www.jstor.org/stable/2231790?origin=JSTOR-pdf&seq=1#page_scan_tab_contents.

3 Andrew Stewart Skinner, ed., *The Glasgow Edition of the Works and Correspondence of Adam Smith*, vol. 2, bk. 2, *Of the Nature, Accumulation, and Employment of Stock* (Oxford: Clarendon Press, 1976–83).

4 W. Arthur Lewis, "Economic Development with Unlimited Supplies of Labor," *The Manchester School* 22, no. 2 (May 1954): 139–91.

5 Gary S. Becker, *Human Capital: A Theoretical and Empirical Analysis, with Special Reference to Education* (Chicago: University of Chicago Press, 1993).

PLACE IN THE AUTHOR'S WORK

KEY POINTS

- Lucas's chief focus throughout his life's work has been to apply mathematical reasoning to basic economic theory, and developing theories to explain areas of macroeconomics* (economic matters at the larger scale).

- His driving approach is assuming the rationality* of actors (those who act after making informed decisions). His Nobel Prize,* given in 1995, was for exploring the implications of rational expectations*—the way people use information to make their best guesses about the future.

- Although it was neither his first great success nor his last, identifying what became known as the Lucas paradox*—that capital does not flow from developed countries to poor countries even though developing countries have lower levels of capital per worker—in "Why Doesn't Capital Flow from Rich to Poor Countries?" remains a milestone in Lucas's career.

Positioning

By the time "Why Doesn't Capital Flow from Rich to Poor Countries?" was published in 1990, Robert E. Lucas Jr. was already one of America's leading economists. He was the John Dewey Distinguished Service Professor at the University of Chicago, the home turf of the Chicago school.* He was editor of one of the senior journals in his field, the *Journal of Political Economy*. His work on rational expectations,* which would lead to his 1995 Nobel Prize, had already appeared 28 years before. His 1988 work on endogenous growth theory,* which accounted for growth within his economic

> ❝ But who can say how the macroeconomic theory of the future will develop, any more than anyone in 1960 could have foreseen the developments I have described in this lecture? All one can be sure of is that progress will result from the continued effort to formulate explicit theories that fit the facts, and that the best and most practical macroeconomics will make use of developments in basic economic theory. ❞
>
> Robert E. Lucas Jr., Nobel Prize lecture, December 1995

model, rather than treating it as an exogenous*—unexplained—factor, had been very well received.

Yet even with all these achievements, the Lucas paradox marked a milestone in Lucas's career. His work on the role of human capital* in explaining growth had already brought together the fields of microeconomics,* where poverty had usually been studied, and macroeconomics,* which usually focused on wealthier countries. "Why Doesn't Capital Flow?" opened up even more new directions in the field of development economics.* It posed questions about world poverty that previously had not been asked within the tradition of the Chicago school, and to which the insights of that tradition had not been applied.

There are other important paradoxes in economics. The eighteenth-century economist Adam Smith* explores the paradox of value: diamonds are less useful than water, but are worth more.[1] The resource curse, or paradox of plenty, points out that countries with abundant natural resources are often poorer than those without.[2]

Most economic paradoxes, when identified, have opened up new fields for research. Lucas suggests four possible answers to his paradox, some to do with human capital, some having more to do with imperfections in the markets (or market failure*), and some involving political risk* in the developing world.* For him, the matter is not just of academic interest; different answers suggest very different things for development policy.

Integration

Lucas's emphasis, both here and in his other works, is less on empirical* scholarship than on theory—that is, modeling the behavior of rational people and organizations, after making assumptions about what goals they are trying to pursue.

Part of this is a reaction by members of the Chicago school against the work of earlier Keynesian* economists, which had been highly empirical. Keynesians, for example, recommend increased government spending during recessions to help stimulate the economy. But Lucas is suspicious of putting too much faith in patterns that emerge from large-scale data; he believes these patterns might reflect particular policies that were in effect at the time, and could lead to inaccurate predictions for the future if those policies changed.

This critique—known as the Lucas critique*[3]—is precisely why Lucas puts as much emphasis as he does on the foundations of individual behavior: the preferences held by people and organizations, and the resources and the technology available to them. If you model these, thinks Lucas, then you can predict how broader-scale behavior will change to adapt to changed policies. And this is why he spends so much effort to bring together microeconomics* and macroeconomics*—he does not think you can reliably analyze the second without the first.

Significance

"Why Doesn't Capital Flow?" remains a classic and hugely influential economic work of the past quarter-century, and has encouraged neoclassical economists* to better engage with questions of world poverty while raising important issues about human capital, market failure, institutions, and corruption and the way in which these have impacted developing countries.

In the tradition of Lucas, whose Lucas paradox generated more than 2,000 subsequent academic studies, researchers have identified other surprising paradoxes. For example, the anti-Lucas paradox* observes that in manufacturing, the capital invested per worker is highest in the poorest countries.

As well as his work on rational expectations and the Lucas paradox, Lucas's best-known, most highly regarded work is the endogenous theory of growth which uses human capital as the thread to stitch together microeconomics and macroeconomics.

Lucas's body of work has been highly influential in academic circles—the number of times his work has been cited confirms this. He has helped steer academic research on rational expectations, capital flow between rich and poor countries, and understanding the role of human capital in growth. While Lucas has now written 5 books and 66 articles, there is no doubt that the Lucas paradox and the Lucas critique form the basis of his academic reputation.

Lucas's influence also extends beyond academia and into the political arena and the media, where he appears in extended interviews for financial journals such as the *Wall Street Journal* and guest columns in the *Economist*. It is little wonder that the *Wall Street Journal* called Robert E. Lucas Jr. "the most influential macroeconomist of the last quarter of the twentieth century."[4]

NOTES

1 Andrew Stewart Skinner, ed., *The Glasgow Edition of the Works and Correspondence of Adam Smith*, vol. 1, bk. 1.4, *Of the Origin and Use of Money* (Oxford: Clarendon Press, 1976–83).

2 Jeffrey D. Sachs and Andrew M. Warner, "Natural Resource Abundance and Economic Growth," National Bureau of Economic Research working paper no. 5398 (December 1995), http://www.nber.org/papers/w5398.

3 Robert E. Lucas Jr., "Econometric Policy Evaluation: A Critique," in *The Phillips Curve and Labor Markets* by Karl Brunner and Allan Meltzer, Carnegie-Rochester Conference Series on Public Policy (New York: American Elsevier, 1976): 19–46.

4 N. Gregory Mankiw, "Back In Demand," *Wall Street Journal* (September 21, 2009).

SECTION 3
IMPACT

THE FIRST RESPONSES

KEY POINTS

- There were four main criticisms of Lucas's "Why Doesn't Capital Flow?" Some critics said that the Lucas paradox* comes from Lucas using purchasing-power parity* to compare prices between countries, which introduces distortions. Purchasing-power parity is a method of determining the relative value of different currencies by looking at the cost of a basket of goods and services from one country to another.

- Others suggested that quick rushes of capital* to the developing world* (other than in the form of foreign direct investment*—investment made in a company in another country) would be dangerous and lead to asset bubbles* (which occur when goods trade at a price greatly higher than their actual value), inflation* (the increase in prices), and currency appreciation* (the increase in value of a currency. When a country's currency appreciates, people tend to buy more imported goods, which can harm the country's economy because then there is less demand for domestic goods).

- A few suggested that the paradox could come simply from people investing broadly to reduce the risk of any single investment, rather than seeking the highest possible return. A handful, as we have seen, criticized Lucas's take on human capital* as too limited.

Criticism

While Robert E. Lucas Jr.'s "Why Doesn't Capital Flow from Rich to Poor Countries?" became an instant sensation in economics circles

> ❝ When focusing on manufacturing ... the initial paradox is actually turned into an anti-Lucas paradox: it is in the poorest countries that the capital output ratio is higher. ❞
>
> Orsetta Causa et al., "Lucas and Anti-Lucas Paradoxes"

and attracted a large readership, his arguments received a mixed reception in some academic circles. Lucas's critics generally came largely from academic backgrounds outside the Chicago school.*

Critics said the Lucas paradox may arise just out of the way Lucas measures the capital-output ratio.* The capital-output ratio describes how much capital is needed to produce an extra unit of output. Economies with low capital-output ratios are efficient, and can make more output using the same capital. The capital-output ratio is highest in poor countries: more capital is needed in the poorest countries than in richer ones to make an extra unit of output.[1]

China, for example, a country with a high capital-output ratio, is a capital exporter—meaning that foreign investments in China are lower than the investments that China makes abroad. India, on the other hand, has a lower capital-output ratio than China and tends to import capital (that is, attract foreign investment).

Lucas relies on purchasing-power parity (comparisons of what the same amount of money can buy in different nations) to calculate the capital-output ratio across countries. But the price of outputs will be lower in lower-income countries, which means the quantity of output will be higher for the same amount of investment. This, critics say, creates an artificially lower capital-output ratio, meaning the productivity of capital in those countries will be systematically overestimated. They say using market prices (that is, not using purchasing-power parity) to make comparisons within each country will produce capital-output ratios that are remarkably similar across countries. And measuring that way instead, the Lucas paradox disappears.[2]

Lucas has also been criticized for assuming that a rapid flow of capital from developed nations to developing nations would be an uncomplicated positive thing. Here, critics have said that he does not distinguish between foreign direct investment* (investment in a particular company) and speculative loans to the country itself. Direct investment is generally safer and more stable—and brings with it benefits to human capital and transfers of knowledge. But large, dangerous loans that a country may not have the capacity to absorb may lead to asset bubbles, inflation, and currency appreciation. Critics point to 1980s Latin America and 1990s Asia as examples of costly financial crises cause by excessive debt.[3]

Another criticism has been that Lucas should have focused more on the relationship between capital and labor* than on the capital-output ratio defined above.[4]

Responses

Much of the response has asked whether Lucas measured the right thing, and in the right way. While many researchers have quantified capital flows by producing figures related to direct investment and investment in a country's financial markets,[5] it has been argued that capital can take more forms than this: flows of human capital might be one interesting example.

Lucas talks about the risk of default (the inability to pay back debts), and treats this as an informational issue or a market failure.* But he does not look at how adverse to risks (or how accepting of them) the investors are. There has been research recently suggesting that investors are extremely risk-averse, and will seek to diversify their risks as much as possible by spreading them among multiple investments.[6] This produces another possible explanation for why capital might stay in the developed world*—investors are not maximizing their returns, but instead maximizing a combination of those returns and a diversity of risk.

Conflict and Consensus

The 2008 financial crisis* led to some criticism of the views of the Chicago school and Robert E. Lucas Jr. The crisis led Lucas to modify his views somewhat about monetarism* (an emphasis on low inflation) and some positions held by the economist Milton Friedman.* As Lucas put it in an interview: "I was [initially] convinced by Friedman and Schwartz that the 1929–33 downturn was induced by monetary factors ... I now believe that the evidence on postwar recessions (up to but not including the one we are now in) overwhelmingly supports the dominant importance of real shocks. But I remain convinced of the importance of financial shocks in the 1930s and the years after 2008. Of course, this means I have to renounce the view that business cycles are all alike!"[7]

There are, then, for Lucas, now two sorts of recessions. One, more frequent and milder, is brought about by "real shocks." Causes include technological innovations, bad weather, imported oil price increase, stricter environmental and safety regulations.[8] Less frequent but harsher are ones caused by "financial shocks"—the Great Depression* and the 2008 crisis being two.

A few authors who thought the Lucas paradox came from mistakenly using purchasing-power parity were surprised to identify what they then called the anti-Lucas paradox*—the fact that, in manufacturing, poor countries turn out to have *more* capital per worker than rich countries![9] The name of the paradox is derived from the Lucas paradox's stipulation that there is *less* capital invested per worker in poor countries—which explains why the marginal returns* of investment should be higher in those countries, and why investment should race there.

These authors go on to suggest that poor countries have more capital per manufacturing worker because private investors have to make up for deficient local infrastructure. If there is no reliable electricity, for example, then investors will need to pay privately for their own electrical generators.

NOTES

1   Dwight H. *Perkins et al.*, *Economics of Development* (New York: W. W. Norton, 2001).

2   Orsetta Causa and Daniel Cohen, "Industrial Productivity in 51 Countries, Rich and Poor," Centre for Economic Policy Research (March 2006).

3   Uri Dadush and Bennett Stancil, "The Capital Flow Conundrum," The Carnegie Endowment for International Peace (June 2011), http://carnegieendowment.org/ieb/2011/06/23/capital-flow-conundrum.

4   Daniel Gros, "Why Does Capital Flow from Poor to Rich Countries?," Centre for European Policy Studies (August 26, 2013), http://www.voxeu.org/article/why-does-capital-flow-poor-rich-countries.

5   Laura Alfaro et al., "FDI and Economic Growth: The Role of Local Financial Markets," *Journal of International Economics* 64, no. 1 (October 2004): 89–112.

6   Maurice Obstfeld and Alan M. Taylor, *Global Capital Markets: Integration, Crisis, and Growth* (New York: Cambridge University Press, 2004).

7   Robert E. Lucas Jr., "Robert Lucas on Modern Macroeconomics," *Economic Dynamics newsletter* 14, no. 1, Society for Economic Dynamics (November 2012).

8   Finn E. Kydland and Edward C. Prescott, "Time to Build and Aggregate Fluctuations," *Econometrica* 50, no. 6 (November 1982), https://www.minneapolisfed.org/~/media/files/research/prescott/papers/timetobuild.pdf?la=en.

9   Orsetta Causa et al., "Lucas and Anti-Lucas Paradoxes," Centre for Economic Policy Research discussion paper no. 6013 (December 13, 2006).

MODULE 10
THE EVOLVING DEBATE

KEY POINTS

- Lucas's argument—that mainstream economics suggests capital* should rush to the developing world*—was largely accepted. This shifted the debate to *why* it does not.

- Two main schools of thought have appeared on the topic, one pursuing research that stresses economic fundamentals (governmental policies and institutions), and the other, market failures.*

- In reality, the reasons behind the Lucas paradox* are likely to be a combination of the factors identified above. Methods of measurement may also play a role.

Uses and Problems

A few scholars have attempted to address a related, extreme example of the question Robert E. Lucas Jr. asks in "Why Doesn't Capital Flow from Rich to Poor Countries?"—why does so much capital, in fact, flow from poor to rich countries?

One answer is that investment opportunities are more common in the developed world.* Emerging markets represent 46 percent of global savings, but only 23 percent of the world stock market, so if investors in the developing world wanted to diversify their investments (in a way proportional to the world portfolio of stocks), they would place 77 percent of their savings in the wealthier countries. This works out to about $2.9 trillion each year of capital flowing from poor countries to rich ones.[1] (A related answer is for investors to place their savings in foreign reserves,* that is, the amount of foreign currency held by central banks, often for the purpose of keeping a country's

> **❝** The Lucas paradox has received a lot of attention as the different explanations behind the puzzle have different and sometimes opposite policy responses. **❞**
>
> Laura Alfaro et al., "Why Doesn't Capital Flow from Rich to Poor Countries? An Empirical Investigation"

own currency more stable. China is one potent example, with its holdings of dollars reaching $4 trillion in August 2014.[2])

Another puzzle that researchers after Lucas have identified is the "allocation puzzle." Capital flows (the movement of money) from rich to poor countries are not only low (the Lucas paradox), but their *distribution* across developing countries is the opposite of what mainstream economics would predict.[3] Textbook models, as we have seen, say that capital should flow to the countries with a higher marginal product of capital, meaning a higher output (that is, what is produced) produced by the next unit of capital (investment). Actually, it does the opposite. For example, productivity in South Korea grew by 4.5 percent each year between 1980 and 2000, and fell 1.1 percent each year in Madagascar. Yet South Korea attracted almost no net capital inflows (meaning the purchase of domestic assets by foreign investors), while Madagascar averaged inflows corresponding to 6 percent of its output.

Schools of Thought

Very broadly, two schools of thought have attempted to address the Lucas paradox—one emphasizing the importance of economic fundamentals (meaning the most basic indices that measure the economic growth rate, inflation and unemployment), and the other school putting more stress on market failures (situations where markets fail to allocate goods and services efficiently).

Economic fundamentals include government policies like tariffs,* taxes, and capital controls (meaning government restrictions to regulate flows of capital in and out of a country), institutions (that is, properly functioning and noncorrupt courts and other structures that protect contracts and property rights), and factors of production (meaning the inputs that produce goods, such as capital, labor, land and entrepreneurship) that may be missing.

Market failures include the risk of sovereign default (a nation's inability to repay its debts) and imperfect information (where the lending country does not have all the facts they need about the borrowing country). Capital in a poor nation may be productive and offer a high marginal rate of return,* as neoclassical economics* might predict, but foreign companies choose not to invest there because the local markets are broken in one way or another.

Some researchers have looked at factors within the rich nations themselves—these can be thought of as external, or push, factors. Researchers have found that low interest rates in wealthy nations, and especially the United States, played an important role during the 1990s in renewing lending to developing countries.[4]

Others have looked to factors within a country—internal, or pull, factors—especially in foreign direct investment.* Government size, political stability, and openness all prove important elements in attracting foreign direct investment.

In Current Scholarship

There has been much recent work exploring different answers to the Lucas paradox.

One argument says repeated defaults by developing countries is key for understanding why so little capital flows to poor countries. Since 1946, the poorest countries defaulted between half and a third of the time, even when the amount borrowed was very small. Some conclude that the answer must lie mainly in political risk:* "the fact that so many poor countries are in default on their debts, that so little funds are channeled through equity, and that overall private lending rises more than proportionally with wealth, all strongly support the view that credit markets and political risk are the main reasons why we do not see more capital flows to developing countries."[5]

Several recent authors suggest that one economic fundamental pull factor—institutional quality—is the strongest explanation for the Lucas paradox between 1971 and 1998.[6] An example is the US technology company Intel's decision concerning where to locate its overseas semiconductor plant in 1996: the company's short list included Costa Rica and Mexico. Mexico, as a larger country, possessed more human capital,* measured by the number of engineers and technically qualified graduates; Costa Rica enjoyed greater stability and less corruption. Intel chose Costa Rica.[7]

Also according to these authors' calculations, improving the quality of Peru's institutions to the level of Australia's should lead to a quadrupling of foreign investment; they pursue Lucas's suggestion that the answer to the Lucas paradox may be different in the periods before and after World War II*—and they tentatively suggest that human capital seems slightly stronger in the years between 1918 and 1945.

And in the tradition of questioning whether the flow of capital to poorer countries is actually required for their development, a paper from 2007 showed that developing countries with less reliance on foreign capital grew faster.[8]

NOTES

1   Uri Dadush and Bennett Stancil, "The Capital Flow Conundrum," The Carnegie Endowment for International Peace (June 2011), http://carnegieendowment.org/ieb/2011/06/23/capital-flow-conundrum.

2   Gavyn Davies, "The Drain on China's Foreign Exchange Reserves," *FT.com* (September 21, 2015), http://blogs.ft.com/gavyndavies/2015/09/21/the-drain-on-chinas-foreign-exchange-reserves/.

3   Pierre-Olivier Gourinchas and Olivier Jeanne, "Capital Flows to Developing Countries: The Allocation Puzzle," *Review of Economic Studies* 80 (January 2013), http://socrates.berkeley.edu/~pog/academic/2013_RESTUD_published.pdf.

4   Guillermo A. Calvo et al., "Inflows of Capital to Developing Countries in the 1990s," *Journal of Economic Perspectives* 10, no. 2 (Spring 1996): 123–39.

5   Carmen M. Reinhart and Kenneth S. Rogoff, "Serial Default and the 'Paradox' of Rich-to-Poor Capital Flows," *American Economic Review* 94, no. 2 (May 2004), **doi:**10.1257/0002828041302370.

6   Laura Alfaro et al., "Why Doesn't Capital Flow from Rich to Poor Countries? An Empirical Investigation," *Review of Economics and Statistics*, 90, no. 2 (May 2008): 347–68.

7   Debora Spar, "Attracting High Technology Investment: Intel's Costa Rican Plant," Foreign Investment Advisory Service occasional paper no. FIAS 11, World Bank (April 1998), http://documents.worldbank.org/curated/en/1998/04/693630/attracting-high-technology-investment-intels-costa-rican-plant.

8   Eswar *Prasad et al.*, "The Paradox of Capital," *Finance & Development* 44, no. 1, IMF (March 2007), http://www.imf.org/external/pubs/ft/fandd/2007/03/prasad.htm.

IMPACT AND INFLUENCE TODAY

KEY POINTS

- "Why Doesn't Capital Flow from Rich to Poor Countries?" remains a key text for anyone interested in capital* movements and economic development.*

- The work challenges the Chicago school* approach to address questions of persistent poverty in the developing world* in a more nuanced fashion than simply prescribing deregulation.* At the same time, it uses the conceptual machinery of neoclassical economics to explore an important aspect of poverty in the developing world: why poorer countries don't attract more investment.

- "Why Doesn't Capital Flow?" has spurred a huge amount of research, including 2,450 results on the popular academic search engine Google Scholar.

Position

Some 25 years after the publication of Robert E. Lucas Jr.'s "Why Doesn't Capital Flow from Rich to Poor Countries?" his scholarly paper is still important for anyone interested in economics and world poverty. This suggests that, despite critiques raised when these ideas first appeared in 1990 and thereafter, the academic community regards Lucas's work favorably.

Capital flows between countries were also affected by the increased influence of certain Keynesian* ideas following the 2008 crisis* (the Keynesian idea of large-scale economic stimulus, or government spending, was a key strategy in responding to that financial crisis). Meanwhile, Keynesian capital controls designed to prevent the flow of capital from a nation—capital controls meaning government

> ❝ Macroeconomics in this original sense has succeeded: its central problem of depression has been solved, for all practical purposes. ❞
>
> Robert E. Lucas Jr. in Robert Skidelsky, "What's Wrong with the Economy – and with Economics?"

restrictions such as taxes on transactions and restrictions on the amount of money one is allowed to take from a nation—have regained some legitimacy in both academic and policy circles. In July 1944, negotiations at Bretton Woods* in the United States led to the founding of the International Monetary Fund* and the World Bank* (global financial institutions that provide aid and loans for developing nations). The economist John Maynard Keynes* had said in 1942 that "control of capital movements, both inward and outward, should be a permanent feature of the post-war system."[1]

But in the 1990s, developing countries began abolishing their capital controls—some to gain entry to the Organization for Economic Cooperation and Development,* an organization founded in 1961 to support trade between countries. Other countries abandoned capital controls as part of bailout agreements with the International Monetary Fund. Wealthy countries had dismantled their capital controls earlier, in the 1980s, but when Lucas wrote "Why Doesn't Capital Flow?" they were still in place in poorer countries. Although Lucas does not directly consider capital controls in his article, they would figure under his discussion of institutions and in his briefly considered possibility that poorer countries do not want richer countries' capital.

Interaction

"Why Doesn't Capital Flow?" is still relevant to a broad range of economic problems. References to the book appear frequently in contexts ranging from equity markets and globalization to human capital.*

It is also worth pointing out that the tools of microeconomic* analysis honed by Robert E. Lucas Jr. and the Chicago school have become important in a wide variety of fields outside economics. Approaches based on maximized utility* (the idea that individuals will make economic choices that will maximize their satisfaction) and equilibrium* (a balanced state of supply and demand, in which no individual can improve an economic outcome without someone else changing their behavior) have been deployed to explain voter turnout, arms control, negotiations between labor* and management, and even drug addiction, computer science, and biology (gender ratios among newborns, and altruism towards family members). The use of the methods to model the strategic behavior of two or more people (or countries or organizations) who interact while each trying to maximize their own utility is called game theory.*

Advocates point to the surprising insights that can be gained from starting with simple assumptions and using mathematics to show the results that follow from them—exactly the method Lucas applied in "Why Doesn't Capital Flow?" Critics say that the simplifications discard too much about human behavior. The debate is a lively one within the academic world in many disciplines across social sciences and beyond.

The Continuing Debate
Lucas suggested the answers to his paradox might change between the eras before and after World War II,* or before and after the 2008 financial crisis. There may be different answers at different times as to why the flow of capital shifts, why some developing economies attract capital and others do not, and why investors sometimes seem to behave irrationally.

Between 2009 and early 2011, a number of developing nations (including Brazil, South Korea, and Taiwan) began to impose capital controls (intended to prevent the flow of capital from a nation) to halt appreciation of their currencies while cooling asset bubbles* (when goods trade at a price higher than the actual value) and inflation* (the overall increase in prices). After the crisis, critics said capital flows had exaggerated the business cycle: at the first sign that a developing country's economy was faltering, international investment exited the country in droves. (The exception was foreign direct investment, which tends to remain in the long-term.) Critics also said that before the downturn, unregulated capital had rushed into many developing countries faster than their economies could absorb it, causing asset bubbles and inflation in countries such as Thailand. During recessions, capital races back to the safer investment haven of the United States and other developed countries.

Capital controls imposed after the 2008 financial crisis* represented a comeback of the Keynesian* emphasis on government intervention in the economy, but the actual effects of capital controls have been more in keeping with the predictions of the Chicago school, which favors free markets. The *Wall Street Journal* wrote in 2015 about Iceland's capital controls: "The restrictions have helped steady the exchange rate and curb inflation, and the central bank predicts growth of 4.5% this year. But the controls remain a headache for Iceland's authorities and businessmen, for whom compliance means a mountain of paperwork and punishing limitations on their ability to invest, expand, and trade."[2]

NOTES

1   Eric Helleiner, *States and the Reemergence of Global Finance: From Bretton Woods to the 1990s* (Ithaca, NY: Cornell University Press, 1994), 33.

2   Charles Duxbury, "For Greece, Iceland Shows Risks of Capital Controls," *Wall Street Journal* (July 3, 2015), http://www.wsj.com/articles/for-greece-iceland-shows-risks-of-capital-controls-1435932791.

WHERE NEXT?

KEY POINTS

- While it is likely that "Why Doesn't Capital Flow?" will continue to be very relevant, its relevance is greater at some points than at others—after the 2008 financial crisis,* for example, when investment rushed out of developing economies.

- At other times—and as some of Lucas's critics have observed—too *much* capital* can flow to developing countries,* producing asset bubbles,* as occurred in the years leading up to 2008.

- But Lucas remains relevant in posing the question of why capital goes to certain countries and not others (such as the very poorest, where the amount of capital is at its lowest compared to the available labor*).

Potential

Robert E. Lucas Jr.'s "Why Doesn't Capital Flow from Rich to Poor Countries?" should offer us a means to analyze, act, and respond to changing economic circumstances.

Foreign direct investment* is when an overseas investor sends money to a particular company rather than to a country's financial markets. It is the most helpful sort of capital, because it is harder to sell off during financial crises, and it leads to technology and knowledge being transferred. It may promote human capital* development through training programs run jointly with the overseas investor. It has been called the "good cholesterol" of capital, compared with the potentially "bad cholesterol" of financial capital.[1] Critics do, however, point out some possible downsides to foreign direct investment. For

> **❝** ... [T]he term 'Lucas critique' has survived, long after that original context has disappeared. It has a life of its own and means different things to different people. Sometimes it is used like a cross you are supposed to use to hold off vampires: just waving it at an opponent defeats him. Too much of this, no matter what side you are on, becomes just name calling." **❞**
>
> Robert E. Lucas Jr., 2012

example, if the investment is geared to serving domestic markets protected by high import tariffs* or other barriers, it may strengthen lobbying efforts to maintain the barriers, which result in a poor allocation of resources.[2]

In the camp of more dangerous capital is what has come to be known as "hot money,"* a term describing speculative capital flows between countries. These are often provoked by less-regulated investment practices and financial institutions, flowing quickly in and out of markets to earn short-term profits on changes in interest rates or exchange rates.

The effect of hot money is observed especially frequently in periods such as the aftermath of the 2008 financial crisis. Before the downturn, the industrialized economies found themselves with very low interest rates (close to zero) and an expanding supply of money. These very low interest rates prompt the wealthier economies to invest in developing countries such as Brazil, India, South Africa, and Turkey that offer higher interest rates and better prospects for growth. The most tempting targets are developing countries like these four that have adopted market-oriented reforms, such as reducing barriers in their trade and capital markets. Each has experienced large inflows of borrowed capital, and their currencies have appreciated faster than elsewhere. The countries grow their economies by depending on the foreign capital, which can cause wrenching problems in a downturn such as in 2008 when the hot money flees to the safe haven of wealthier nations.

Future Directions

It seems likely that the Lucas paradox* will always have a place among the most influential economics ideas. Students of capital flows and development* will continue to find "Why Doesn't Capital Flow?" a "must-read." Indeed, even 25 years after its publication, many attempts are being made to solve the paradox with fresh research. The article's title has become one of the great economic questions.

"Why Doesn't Capital Flow?" is relevant to such pressing issues as the huge foreign reserve levels of China and other developing countries in Asia—the result of capital flowing the other way, from poor countries to rich countries. And with governments, markets, and international financial institutions now more aware of the dangers posed by overly rapid capital flow surges, it is more important than ever to understand exactly what attracts capital, and when.

For years to come, policy-makers and academics alike will continue trying to understand the difference between helpful and dangerous capital, and how to encourage the sort of capital investment that is better for developing poorer nations.

More recent economists, such as Amartya Sen* of India, have shared the Chicago school's* view that free markets are essential in achieving development. But Sen and others also stress the need for institutional mechanisms to ensure political freedoms and open, trustworthy financial systems. The necessary factors include freedom of opportunity, including an ability to access credit, as well as income supplements and unemployment benefits to provide freedom from extreme poverty.*[3]

Summary

"Why Doesn't Capital Flow?" will undoubtedly continue to be a seminal text for many years.

The fact that there is no simple answer to the Lucas paradox after decades of analysis suggests that policy-makers, academics, and the informed public need to think with greater clarity about what, at the microeconomic* level, drives capital flows between rich and poor nations at the macroeconomic* level.

While Lucas is motivated by concern to see more investment reach the poorest countries, so enabling them to grow, the 2008 financial crisis has led economists, governments, and global development organizations including the World Bank* and International Monetary Fund* to differentiate between helpful and dangerous capital.

Researchers have applied the concept of the Lucas paradox in such different fields as colonization,*[4] "brain drain,"*[5] (the flow of human capital from one nation to another) and technology transfer (the process of transferring technologies between countries to a secondary user. A scholarly paper published in January 2015 was titled "Why Doesn't Technology Flow from Rich to Poor Countries?")[6]

"Why Doesn't Capital Flow?" is especially relevant to policy-makers for its policy implications. In the future, as a great unsolved question, the Lucas paradox will continue to provoke new scholarship on the important questions of capital investment in the poorest countries.

NOTES

1   Ricardo Hausmann and Eduardo Fernández-Arias, "Foreign Direct Investment: Good Cholesterol?" Inter-American Development Bank working paper no. 417 (March 2000).

2   Prakash Loungani and Assaf Razin, "How Beneficial is Foreign Direct Investment for Developing Countries?" *Finance & Development* 38, no. 2, IMF (June 2001).

3   Amartya Sen, *Development as Freedom* (Oxford: Oxford University Press, 1999).

4   Graziella Bertocchi and Fabio Canova, "Did Colonization Matter for Growth?: An Empirical Exploration into the Historical Causes of Africa's Underdevelopment," *European Economic Review* 46, no. 10 (December 2002): 1851–71.

5   Thomas Straubhaar, "International Mobility of the Highly Skilled: Brain Gain, Brain Drain, or Brain Exchange," Hamburg Institute of International Economics (HWWA) discussion paper 88 (2000), http://www.econstor.eu/handle/10419/19463.

6   Harold L. Cole et al., "Why Doesn't Technology Flow from Rich to Poor Countries?" National Bureau of Economic Research working paper no. 20856 (January 2015).

GLOSSARY

GLOSSARY OF TERMS

Anti-Lucas paradox: the paradox, identified in 2006, that in manufacturing, poor countries have more capital per worker than rich countries.

Asset bubble: the situation that arises when goods trade at a price greatly higher than their actual value. Explanations have included uncertainty, speculation, and decision-making limited by incomplete information, time, or capacity to make optimal decisions. Housing markets from 2006 in the United States, Britain, and Ireland and Internet startups in California's Silicon Valley from 1995 to 2000 are commonly used examples of asset bubbles.

Balance of trade: A nation's gap between the value of its exports and that of its imports. If positive it is a trade surplus; if negative, a trade deficit.

Brain drain: the flight of human capital, and emigration of highly skilled individuals, in pursuit of improved pay, conditions, and opportunities.

Bretton Woods Conference: a conference held in July 1944 in the US state of New Hampshire that laid the foundations for the economic order following World War II, including convertible currencies (that is, without government restrictions) with fixed exchange rates, and established the World Bank and International Monetary Fund. John Maynard Keynes was the principal British negotiator.

Bullion: precious metals, chiefly gold and silver.

Capital: money or human skill used in productive economic activity. Along with land and labor, it is one of the three factors of production.

Capital-output ratio: the amount of capital needed to produce an output over time. (Often the output is growth of the gross domestic product—that is, the monetary value of goods and services produced in a country over a specified time.) When capital is more abundant than other inputs (such as natural resources), the proportion of capital tends to be higher.

Chicago school: a school within neoclassical economics associated with academics and former students of the University of Chicago's department of economics. Key figures include Milton Friedman, George Stigler, Gary Becker, and Robert E. Lucas Jr. Their policy prescriptions have typically included free-market policies and government efforts aimed at price stability, which were criticized after the 2008 financial crisis.

Classical economics: a tradition of economics often held to begin with Adam Smith's 1776 *The Wealth of Nations*, which prescribes free markets and a hands-off policy from governments.

Cobb-Douglas production function: this shows the relationship between capital and labor in making production, and the value of goods made. It was named for Charles Cobb and Paul Douglas, who developed and tested it between 1927 and 1947.

Cold War: a period of prolonged struggle between the United States and Soviet Union and their associated blocs following World War II and ending with the dissolution of the Soviet Union in 1991.

Collective bargaining: Negotiations over pay and workplace conditions, typically taking place between a trade union and management. The rights of workers to form trade unions and bargain collectively with employers are protected in the United States by the

National Labor Relations Act of 1935, and in Britain by the Trade Union and Labour Relations (Consolidation) Act 1992.

Colonial: a period of history, and set of relationships, in which several European nations established colonies in Asia, Africa, and the Americas. Imperialism began in the sixteenth century and was associated with ideas of mercantilism. With the exception of a few small remaining overseas territories governed by European states, the colonial period ended in the aftermath of World War II.

Conditionality: the use of conditions by the International Monetary Fund, World Bank, or a donor nation, that a nation must meet in order to receive aid, a loan, or relief on its debts.

Currency appreciation: a currency appreciates when its value increases relative to other currencies—often through increased exports, employment, or interest rates. The opposite is depreciation, when its value diminishes.

Democracy: a political system in which free and fair elections select the government, and there are effective protections for citizens' rights and the rule of law.

Democratic Party: the largest center-left political party in the United States, founded in 1828. Democrat presidents have included Bill Clinton, John F. Kennedy, and Barack Obama.

Dependency theory: a school of development thought that says poorer (or periphery) countries are permanently disadvantaged by wealthier (or core) countries that purchase their raw materials, use their cheap labor, and sell them the finished products. It is a reaction against W. W. Rostow's modernization theory that viewed all societies as passing through the same stages of development. Hans Singer and Raúl Prebisch were early and important thinkers in the dependency theory tradition.

Deregulation: the reduction of government rules or oversight (supervision) in the economy, and a policy prescription of Chicago school economists. Deregulation was a heavy feature of the economic programs of President Reagan in the United States and the British prime minister Margaret Thatcher.

Developed world: the world's wealthier, economically developed countries. During the Cold War, the term First World was used to describe North America, Western Europe, Australasia, and Japan. The Second World described the world's Communist nations, and the Third World the generally postcolonial, nonaligned states.

Developing world: the poorer nations of Africa, Asia, and Latin America, many of which gained independence after World War II. The term Third World, used to describe these nations, originated during the Cold War.

Development: within economics, a subfield focusing chiefly on poorer countries, and measures or reforms aimed at raising their standard of living.

Diminishing returns: a principle within economics which states that there is a point after adding more of a factor of production—extra workers at a factory, for example, or seed on a farm's field—when the output will be less than the output following similar additions earlier on in the process of production

Egalitarian: an ideology or institution that tends to treat all people as equals.

Empirical: an approach in economics that analyzes behavior in the real world, often through statistics. The other principal approach, theoretical work, concentrates instead on predicting and explaining relationships between variables. Much research combines both approaches.

Endogenous growth theory: a model of economic growth that treats growth as the result of investment in innovation and knowledge, rather than as an exogenous (unexplained) variable (typically the fluctuating savings rate or the rate of technical progress).

Equilibrium: if there is perfect competition, equilibrium takes place when supply and demand are balanced, and a price is set that will lead to the amount demanded being the same as the quantity supplied.

Exogenous factors: variables that come from outside an economic model, and are not explained by the model.

Extreme poverty: the standard of living of 1.2 billion people existing on less than $1.25 a day (measured, because of Western inflation, in 2005 dollars).

Financial crisis of 2008: a global economic downturn that saw a worldwide drop in stock markets, many banks needing to be rescued by governments, and unemployment and drops in housing markets. The decline lasted until 2012.

Foreign direct investment: investment made in a company in another country.

Foreign reserves: reserves held by central banks in a currency or basket of currencies, typically comprising the dollar, euro, pound sterling, and yen.

Game theory: a field that seeks to model interactions of conflict and cooperation between different people, institutions, or countries that have clear goals and behave rationally but act under conditions of uncertainty.

Great Depression: a worldwide period of economic distress that saw world GDP (gross domestic product, a measure of the size of an economy based on the value of goods and services produced during a specified time period) fall 15% from 1929 to 1932, and unemployment rise to 25 percent in the United States and elsewhere, such as the northeast of England, as high as 70 percent.

Hot money: speculative capital flows between countries, especially to earn short-term profits on fluctuations in interest rates or exchange rates.

Human capital: the economic resource consisting of the education, knowledge, and skills possessed by an individual (rather than their actual work, which is labor). The concept was further developed by Jacob Mincer and Gary Becker of the Chicago school.

Import-substitution industrialization: attempts by a country to replace imported goods and services with locally produced ones. Particularly popular in Latin America from the 1950s onwards, such attempts were largely abandoned in the 1980s and 1990s in favor of more free-market policies.

Inflation: the increase over time in the level of prices in an economy.

International capital market: markets where savers lend money, by buying stocks and bonds, to countries and companies that can provide a return on investment.

International Monetary Fund (IMF): an organization founded after World War II to prevent the spread of international economic crises and oversee the world monetary and financial system.

Keynesian economics: a school of economic thought that began during the Great Depression, following the work of John Maynard Keynes. Notably, it suggests that governments should engage in deficit spending during recessions. It lost influence during the economic slowdown of the 1970s, but has had some resurgence since 2008.

Labor: the human effort used in production, alongside capital and land.

Lucas critique: the argument made by Lucas in 1976 that it is naïve to predict how large-scale economic behavior will adapt to a change in policy from looking at patterns in historical data, as patterns will change when policy changes.

Lucas paradox: the puzzle, identified by Lucas in 1990, that we do not observe capital to move from wealthy countries to poor ones, despite the fact that there are lower levels of capital invested per worker in developing countries. Under the law of diminishing returns (when the level of profit is less than the amount of capital invested), investors should expect more returns from their capital when there are lower levels of capital invested per worker.

Macroeconomics: the branch of economics dealing with national, regional, and global economies, and indicators including gross domestic product, unemployment rates, and inflation.

Marginal returns: the change in output from the last unit of input. For example, if you have five workers on an assembly line, the marginal return is the added product you will gain from hiring a sixth. The law of diminishing returns states that there is a point after which further added inputs will lead to a decrease in marginal returns: the ninety-eighth worker may not make as much of a difference as the sixth.

Market failure: situations where markets fail to allocate goods and services efficiently. This could be because of imperfect information, or externalities (third party effects).

Maximized utility: utility represents satisfaction, and microeconomists assume individuals will choose the behavior leading to the highest expected utility. This assumption is called "rational choice."

Mercantilism: a theory in the fifteenth to eighteenth centuries that emphasized a positive balance of trade, and aimed to accumulate monetary reserves chiefly in the form of gold and silver, by exporting more than the level of imports. High tariffs, banning export of bullion, and subsidies on exports, were frequent features of mercantilism.

Microeconomics: a branch of economics that looks at individuals and firms and their decision-making.

Monetarism: a school of thought principally associated with Milton Friedman, and developed in his 1963 book (cowritten with Anna Jacobson Schwartz) *A Monetary History of the United States, 1867–1960*. It holds that the main task of governments is to ensure low inflation (price stability) by focusing on a slow expansion of the supply of money.

Monopoly: when one supplier (often a company) controls the supply of a good or service that does not have a close substitute, and can set its price higher than would otherwise be possible.

Moral hazard: the risk that an actor—for instance, a developing nation that has borrowed capital internationally in a loan—will have an incentive to engage in riskier behavior, because another party (in this case, the investor) bears the risk.

New Deal: a set of domestic policies implemented by President Franklin D. Roosevelt in the United States between 1933 and 1938, in response to the Great Depression. They included deficit spending to speed America's economic recovery.

Neoclassical economics: a set of twentieth-century approaches to economics (mainly microeconomics) that build on the tradition of classical economics by focusing on concepts such as marginal returns, maximized utility and equilibrium. Neoclassical economics is the dominant form in today's global economy.

Nobel Prize in Economics: the Nobel Memorial Prize in Economic Sciences has been awarded annually since 1969. It is the most prestigious award in the field of economics.

Organization for Economic Cooperation and Development: an organization of 34 countries founded in 1961 to promote trade and development. Most members are high-income, developed countries.

Political risk: within economics, political risks principally refer to the possibility that an investment or loan could suffer because of political instability or government decisions in a country. For example, a new government may be elected that chooses to repudiate all of a country's overseas debts.

Price theory: a body of work looking into how prices are set by the interaction between supply and demand. This was also a significant series of courses taught by Milton Friedman to postgraduates at the University of Chicago.

Purchasing-power parity (PPP): a way to determine the relative value of different currencies. It looks at the cost of a basket of goods and services from one country to another, rather than market exchange rates of currencies. The GDP (gross domestic product) of India in 2015 was $1,704 in US dollars by market exchange values, but $3,608 using purchasing-power parity.

Rational expectations: a field of research that investigates how people make best guesses about the future, under uncertainty, by using all available information.

Rationality: contemporary economics makes assumptions about the behavior of people and organizations. First, that they will adopt the best actions to achieve their goals. Second, that their preferences and beliefs will be consistent. And third, that they will make full use of the information they have. These assumptions collectively are the basis of what is called rational choice scholarship.

Republican Party: the largest right-wing party in the United States, founded in 1854. Republican presidents include George W. Bush, Herbert Hoover, and Richard Nixon.

Solow model (or Solow–Swan model): a model of economic growth over the long term, set in the framework of neoclassical economics, and developed by Robert Solow in 1956. It explains growth in terms of capital accumulation, population growth, and increases in productivity from technological progress.

Sovereign default: the failure of a state to fully repay its debts. If international lenders fear that a country may default, they may require higher interest rates for future loans.

Soviet Union: a federation of communist states that existed between 1922 and 1991, centered primarily on Russia and its neighbors in Eastern Europe and the northern half of Asia.

Stages of growth theory: an influential model of economic development devised in 1960 by American economist W.W. Rostow, this theory states that all countries will pass through five stages: traditional society, conditions prior to takeoff, takeoff, a drive to maturity, and high mass consumption. Rostow argued that takeoff must occur in the sectors in which the country enjoys a comparative advantage over other countries.

Subsidies: government help to a sector, business, or consumer, in support of aspects such as prices in a sector, or a reduction in the price of goods to a consumer. Because subsidies represent an interference in the market, the Chicago school encourages governments not to make them.

Tariffs: a tax on imports (or occasionally exports) that is used in import-substitution industrialization to make overseas products artificially more expensive than domestically produced ones. Such tariffs have been used since the Middle Ages. Tariffs, like subsidies, are discouraged by the Chicago school, and are out of favor within mainstream economics.

Theoretical: an approach within economics that makes predictions based on assumptions about the preferences of individuals and organizations. The other principal approach, empirical work, looks at behavior in the actual world, often through statistics. Much research combines both approaches.

Union: an organization of workers who come together to bargain collectively with employers. The first unions began in eighteenth-century Britain, and spread to other industrializing countries in the late nineteenth century.

World Bank: an international financial institution, founded alongside the International Monetary Fund in 1944, to provide loans to developing countries.

World War II: the deadliest global conflict in human history. It ran from 1939 to 1945, involved the majority of the world's nations, and resulted in between 50 and 85 million fatalities. Wartime devastation of Europe led to the emergence of the United States as the world's largest economy and, jointly with the Soviet Union, its foremost power.

PEOPLE MENTIONED IN THE TEXT

Laura Alfaro is the Warren Alpert Professor of Business Administration at the Harvard Business School, and a former government minister in Costa Rica.

Kenneth J. Arrow (b. 1921) is an American economist in the neoclassical tradition, who received the Nobel Prize in Economics in 1972. He is perhaps best known for his impossibility theorem, which shows that when voters are asked to give three or more distinct preferences, a clear order of preferences cannot be determined.

Gary Becker (1930–2014) was an American economist at the University of Chicago, and recipient of the Nobel Prize in Economics in 1992. A member of the Chicago school, he was among the first to use economic frameworks to explain broader topics such as racial discrimination, drug addiction, and family organization. He also contributed important work to the study of human capital.

Orsetta Causa is an Italian-born economist at the Organization for Economic Development.

Charles Cobb (1875–1949) was an economist who lectured at Amherst College, and collaborated on the Cobb-Douglas model with Paul Douglas.

Daniel Cohen (b. 1953) is a French economist at the École d'économie de Paris.

Paul Douglas (1892–1976) was an economist at the University of Chicago, who served as a US senator from Illinois and was a wartime hero in the Marine Corps. In economics he is chiefly known for the

Cobb-Douglas production function, still used in research today.

Milton Friedman (1912–2006) was an economist at the University of Chicago and a pivotal figure in the Chicago school, an advisor to President Reagan and British Prime Minister Margaret Thatcher. He was best known for his work in monetarism and received the Nobel Prize in Economics in 1976.

Lyndon B. Johnson (1908–73) was the 36th president of the United States. A Democrat, he held office from 1963 to 1969.

John F. Kennedy (1917–63) was the 35th president of the United States. A Democrat, he held the office from January 1961 until his assassination in Dallas on November 22, 1963.

John Maynard Keynes (1883–1946) was a British economist best known for his view that government intervention was needed to balance out cycles in a nation's economy. The school of thought he founded, Keynesian economics, is the principal alternative to the Chicago school.

Frank Knight (1885–1972) was a University of Chicago economist and a founder of the Chicago school. He is best known for his work distinguishing risk and uncertainty and received the Francis A. Walker Medal in 1957, awarded until the Nobel Prize for Economics was created in 1969.

Sir William Arthur Lewis (1915–91) was an economist from Saint Lucia who lectured in Manchester, the West Indies, and Princeton. He is noted for the Lewis model of how countries move from subsistence to industrialization, and for his research in development. He won the Nobel Prize in Economics in 1979.

Jacob Mincer (1922–2006) was a Polish-born economist at Columbia University, and an important labor economist. A member of the Chicago school, he developed the empirical foundations of human capital together with Gary Becker.

Isma'il Pasha (1830–95) was the Khedive, or colonial ruler, of Egypt and Sudan from 1863. While he did much to modernize both countries during his reign, he incurred very sizable debts in construction of the Suez Canal and war with Ethiopia, leading Britain and France to depose him in 1879.

Raúl Prebisch (1901–86) was an Argentinian economist. His (jointly credited alongside German economist Hans Singer) Singer–Prebisch thesis lay at the core of dependency theory, an alternative approach to neoclassical economics which argued that peripheral (developing) countries were permanently disadvantaged by core (developed) ones.

P.V. Narasimha Rao (1921–2004) was the 10th Prime Minister of India from 1991 to 1996. He is principally known for dismantling the socialist policies of his predecessor Rajiv Gandhi and the "License Raj" of India's planned economy, and implementing the reforms called for by the International Monetary Fund.

Ronald Reagan (1911–2004) was president of the United States from 1981 to 1989, and a supporter of deregulation and free markets.

Franklin Delano Roosevelt (1882–1945) was the 32nd president of the United States from 1933 to 1945. He is chiefly known for overseeing an expansion of the government's role during the Great Depression through relief and public works programs designed to generate employment. In 1944, he oversaw the basis for the postwar global economic architecture at the Bretton Woods Conference.

Walt Whitman Rostow (1916–2003) was an economist and government official who served as national security advisor to President Lyndon Johnson from 1966 to 1969. As an economist he is best known for his 1960 *The Stages of Economic Growth*, which argued that all nations' economic development passes through the five same stages.

Paul Samuelson (1915–2009) was the first American to receive the Nobel Prize in Economics in 1970. He worked primarily in what is called the neo-Keynesian tradition. He wrote a weekly column for *Newsweek* with Milton Friedman, where each presented opposing sides of an economic issue of the day.

Amartya Sen (b. 1933) is an Indian-born economist, based chiefly at Harvard and the University of Cambridge. He is known for his book *Development as Freedom* and his work in the economic measurement of poverty and inequality, which has influenced the annual United Nations *Human Development Report*.

Hans Singer (1910–2006) was a German-born British economist and UN official known for his contributions to development economics and dependency theory.

Robert Skidelsky (b. 1939) is a British intellectual historian known principally for his three-volume biography of John Maynard Keynes.

Adam Smith (1723–90) is often considered the father of modern economics, best known for his 1776 book *The Wealth of Nations*. There he argued that in a free market, self-interested competition by individuals benefits all of society by keeping prices low, and providing incentive for a broad range of goods and services.

Robert Solow (b. 1924) is an American economist at the

Massachusetts Institute of Technology and recipient of the Nobel Prize in 1987. He is known particularly for the neoclassical exogenous model of economic growth that bears his name.

Marcelo Soto (b. 1970) is a Chilean economist at the Institute for Economic Analysis in Barcelona.

Margaret Thatcher (1925–2013) was prime minister of the United Kingdom from 1979 to 1990, and, like Ronald Reagan, championed free enterprise.

Vadym Volosovych is a Ukrainian-born international finance academic at Erasmus University Rotterdam.

WORKS CITED

WORKS CITED

Alfaro, Laura, Areendam Chanda, Sebnem Kalemli-Ozcan, and Selin Sayek. "FDI and Economic Growth: The Role of Local Financial Markets." *Journal of International Economics* 64, no. 1 (October 2004): 89–112.

Alfaro, Laura, Sebnem Kalemli-Ozcan, and Vadym Volosovych. "Why Doesn't Capital Flow from Rich to Poor Countries? An Empirical Investigation." *Review of Economics and Statistics* 90, no. 2 (May 2008): 347–68.

Arrow, Kenneth. "The Economic Implications of Learning by Doing." *Review of Economic Studies* 29, no. 3 (June 1962): 155–73. http://www.jstor.org/stable/2295952?seq=1#page_scan_tab_contents.

Becker, Gary S. *Human Capital: A Theoretical and Empirical Analysis, with Special Reference to Education*. Chicago: University of Chicago Press, 1993.

Bertocchi, Graziella, and Fabio Canova. "Did Colonization Matter for Growth?: An Empirical Exploration into the Historical Causes of Africa's Underdevelopment." *European Economic Review* 46, no. 10 (December 2002): 1851–71.

Calvo, Guillermo A., Leonardo Leiderman, and Carmen M. Reinhart. "Inflows of Capital to Developing Countries in the 1990s." *Journal of Economic Perspectives* 10, no. 2 (1996): 123–39.

Causa, Orsetta, and Daniel Cohen. "Industrial Productivity in 51 Countries, Rich and Poor." Centre for Economic Policy Research (March 2006).

Causa, Orsetta, Daniel Cohen, and Marcelo Soto. "Lucas and Anti-Lucas Paradoxes." Centre for Economic Policy Research discussion paper no. 6013 (December 13, 2006).

Cobb, Charles W., and Paul H. Douglas. "A Theory of Production." *American Economic Review* 18, no. 1, supplement (March 1928): 139–65. http://www2.econ.iastate.edu/classes/econ521/orazem/Papers/cobb-douglas.pdf.

Cole, Harold L., Jeremy Greenwood, and Juan M. Sanchez. "Why Doesn't Technology Flow from Rich to Poor Countries?" National Bureau of Economic Research working paper no. 20856 (January 2015).

Dadush, Uri, and Bennett Stancil. "The Capital Flow Conundrum." The Carnegie Endowment for International Peace (June 2011). http://carnegieendowment.org/ieb/2011/06/23/capital-flow-conundrum.

Davies, Gavyn. "The Drain on China's Foreign Exchange Reserves." *FT.com* (September 21, 2015). http://blogs.ft.com/gavyndavies/2015/09/21/the-drain-on-chinas-foreign-exchange-reserves/.

Denison, Edward. *The Sources of Economic Growth in the United States*. New York Committee for Economic Development, 1962.

Duxbury, Charles. "For Greece, Iceland Shows Risk of Capital Controls." *Wall Street Journal* (July 3, 2015). http://www.wsj.com/articles/for-greece-iceland-shows-risks-of-capital-controls-1435932791.

EconTalk. Hosted by Russ Roberts, with Bob Lucas. "Lucas on Growth, Poverty, and Business Cycles." Econtalk (February 5, 2007). http://www.econtalk.org/archives/2007/02/lucas_on_growth.html.

Feldstein, Martin, and Charles Horioka. "Domestic Saving and International Capital Flows." *Economic Journal* 90, no. 358 (1980): 314–29. http://www.jstor.org/stable/2231790?origin=JSTOR-pdf&seq=1#page_scan_tab_contents.

Frängsmyr, Tore, ed. *Les Prix Nobel: The Nobel Prizes 1995*. Stockholm: Nobel Foundation, 1996.

French, Kenneth R., and James M. Poterba. "Investor Diversification and International Equity Markets." *American Economic Review* 81, no. 2 (1991): 222–6. http://www.nber.org/papers/w3609.

Friedman, Milton. "The Real Lesson of Hong Kong." *National Review* (December 31, 1997).

Gourinchas, Pierre-Olivier, and Olivier Jeanne. "Capital Flows to Developing Countries: The Allocation Puzzle." *Review of Economic Studies* 80 (January 2013). http://socrates.berkeley.edu/~pog/academic/2013_RESTUD_published.pdf.

Gros, Daniel. "Why Does Capital Flow from Poor to Rich Countries?" Centre for European Policy Studies (August 26, 2013). http://www.voxeu.org/article/why-does-capital-flow-poor-rich-countries.

Hausmann, Ricardo, and Eduardo Fernández-Arias. "Foreign Direct Investment: Good Cholesterol?" Inter-American Development Bank working paper no. 417 (March 2000).

Helleiner, Eric. *States and the Reemergence of Global Finance: From Bretton Woods to the 1990s*. Ithaca, NY: Cornell University Press, 1994.

Kydland, Finn E. and Edward C. Prescott. "Time to Build and Aggregate Fluctuations." *Econometrica* 50, no. 6 (November 1982). https://www.minneapolisfed.org/~/media/files/research/prescott/papers/timetobuild.pdf?la=en.

Lau, Lawrence J., Dean T. Jamison and Frederic F. Louat. "Education and Productivity in Developing Countries: An Aggregate Production Function Approach." World Bank policy research working paper WPS612 (March 31, 1991).

Lewis, W. Arthur. "Economic Development with Unlimited Supplies of Labor." *The Manchester School* 22, no. 2 (1954): 139–91.

Loungani, Prakash, and Assaf Razin. "How Beneficial is Foreign Direct Investment for Developing Countries?" *Finance & Development* 38, no. 2, IMF (June 2001).

Lucas, Robert E., Jr. "Econometric Policy Evaluation: A Critique." In *The Phillips Curve and Labor Markets* by Karl Brunner and Allan Meltzer. Carnegie-Rochester Conference Series on Public Policy. New York: American Elsevier, 1976.

_____. "Expectations and the Neutrality of Money." *Journal of Economic Theory* 4, no. 2 (April 1972): 103–24.

_____. "On the Mechanics of Economic Development." *Journal of Monetary Economics* 22 (1988): 3–42. http://www.parisschoolofeconomics.eu/docs/darcillon-thibault/lucasmechanicseconomicgrowth.pdf.

_____. "Robert Lucas on Modern Macroeconomics." *Economic Dynamics newsletter* 14, no. 1, Society for Economic Dynamics (November 2012).

_____. "Why Doesn't Capital Flow from Rich to Poor Countries?" *American Economic Review* 80 (1990): 92–6.

Mankiw, N. Gregory. "Back In Demand." *Wall Street Journal* (September 21, 2009). http://www.wsj.com/articles/SB10001424052970204518504574417810281734756.

Nelson, Richard R., and Edmund S. Phelps. "Investment in Humans, Technological Diffusion and Economic Growth." *American Economic Association Papers and Proceedings* 56, no. 2 (1966): 69–75.

Nobel Prize biography. http://www.nobelprize.org/nobel_prizes/economic-sciences/laureates/1995/lucas-bio.html.

Obstfeld, Maurice, and Alan M. Taylor. *Global Capital Markets: Integration, Crisis, and Growth*. Cambridge: Cambridge University Press 2004.

Perkins, Dwight H., Steven C. *Radelet*, Donald R. *Snodgrass*, Malcolm *Gillis* and Michael Roemer. *Economics of Development*. New York: W. W. Norton, 2000.

Prasad, Eswar, Raghuram Rajan, and Arvind Subramanian. "The Paradox of Capital." *Finance & Development* 44, no. 1, IMF (March 2007). http://www.imf.org/external/pubs/ft/fandd/2007/03/prasad.htm.

Reinhart, Carmen, and Kenneth Rogoff. "Serial Default and the 'Paradox' of Rich-to-Poor Capital Flows." *American Economic Review* 94, no. 2 (May 2004). doi: 10.1257/0002828041302370.

Romer, Paul M. "Mathiness in the Theory of Economic Growth." *American Economic Review* 105, no. 5 (2015): 89–93. doi=10.1257/aer.p20151066.

Sachs, Jeffrey D. and Andrew M. Warner. "Natural Resource Abundance and Economic Growth." National Bureau of Economic Research working paper no.

5398 (December 1995). http://www.nber.org/papers/w5398.

Samuelson, Paul A. *Foundations of Economic Analysis*. Cambridge: Harvard University Press, 1983.

Schularick, Moritz. "A Tale of Two 'Globalizations': Capital Flows from Rich to Poor in Two Eras of Global Finance." *International Journal of Finance and Economics* 11 (2006): 339–54. doi:10.1002/ijfe.302.

Sen, Amartya. *Development as Freedom*. Oxford: Oxford University Press, 1999.

Skidelsky, Robert. "The Mystery of Growth." *New York Review of Books* (March 13, 2003). http://www.nybooks.com/articles/2003/03/13/the-mystery-of-growth/.

_____. "What's Wrong with the Economy – and with Economics?" *New York Review of Books* (March 2015). http://www.nybooks.com/daily/2015/03/29/whats-wrong-with-the-economy/.

Solow, Robert M. "A Contribution to the Theory of Economic Growth." *Quarterly Journal of Economics* 70, no. 1 (February 1956): 65–94. http://www.jstor.org/stable/1884513?origin=JSTOR-pdf&seq=1#page_scan_tab_contents.

Spar, Debora. *Attracting High Technology Investment: Intel's Costa Rican Plant*. Foreign Investment Advisory Service occasional paper no. FIAS 11, World Bank (April 1998). http://documents.worldbank.org/curated/en/1998/04/693630/attracting-high-technology-investment-intels-costa-rican-plant.

Stewart Skinner, Andrew, ed., *The Glasgow Edition of the Works and Correspondence of Adam Smith*. Oxford: Clarendon Press, 1976–83.

Straubhaar, Thomas. "International Mobility of the Highly Skilled: Brain Gain, Brain Drain, or Brain Exchange." Hamburg Institute of International Economics (HWWA) discussion paper 88 (2000). http://www.econstor.eu/handle/10419/19463.

Summers, Robert, and Alan Heston. "A New Set of International Comparisons of Real Product and Price Levels: Estimates for 130 Countries, 1950–85." *Review of Income and* Wealth 34, no. 1 (March 1988): 1–25. doi:10.1111/j.1475-4991.1988.tb00558.x.

THE MACAT LIBRARY
BY DISCIPLINE

The Macat Library By Discipline

AFRICANA STUDIES

Chinua Achebe's *An Image of Africa: Racism in Conrad's Heart of Darkness*
W. E. B. Du Bois's *The Souls of Black Folk*
Zora Neale Huston's *Characteristics of Negro Expression*
Martin Luther King Jr's *Why We Can't Wait*
Toni Morrison's *Playing in the Dark: Whiteness in the American Literary Imagination*

ANTHROPOLOGY

Arjun Appadurai's *Modernity at Large: Cultural Dimensions of Globalisation*
Philippe Ariès's *Centuries of Childhood*
Franz Boas's *Race, Language and Culture*
Kim Chan & Renée Mauborgne's *Blue Ocean Strategy*
Jared Diamond's *Guns, Germs & Steel: the Fate of Human Societies*
Jared Diamond's *Collapse: How Societies Choose to Fail or Survive*
E. E. Evans-Pritchard's *Witchcraft, Oracles and Magic Among the Azande*
James Ferguson's *The Anti-Politics Machine*
Clifford Geertz's *The Interpretation of Cultures*
David Graeber's *Debt: the First 5000 Years*
Karen Ho's *Liquidated: An Ethnography of Wall Street*
Geert Hofstede's *Culture's Consequences: Comparing Values, Behaviors, Institutes and Organizations across Nations*
Claude Lévi-Strauss's *Structural Anthropology*
Jay Macleod's *Ain't No Makin' It: Aspirations and Attainment in a Low-Income Neighborhood*
Saba Mahmood's *The Politics of Piety: The Islamic Revival and the Feminist Subject*
Marcel Mauss's *The Gift*

BUSINESS

Jean Lave & Etienne Wenger's *Situated Learning*
Theodore Levitt's *Marketing Myopia*
Burton G. Malkiel's *A Random Walk Down Wall Street*
Douglas McGregor's *The Human Side of Enterprise*
Michael Porter's *Competitive Strategy: Creating and Sustaining Superior Performance*
John Kotter's *Leading Change*
C. K. Prahalad & Gary Hamel's *The Core Competence of the Corporation*

CRIMINOLOGY

Michelle Alexander's *The New Jim Crow: Mass Incarceration in the Age of Colorblindness*
Michael R. Gottfredson & Travis Hirschi's *A General Theory of Crime*
Richard Herrnstein & Charles A. Murray's *The Bell Curve: Intelligence and Class Structure in American Life*
Elizabeth Loftus's *Eyewitness Testimony*
Jay Macleod's *Ain't No Makin' It: Aspirations and Attainment in a Low-Income Neighborhood*
Philip Zimbardo's *The Lucifer Effect*

ECONOMICS

Janet Abu-Lughod's *Before European Hegemony*
Ha-Joon Chang's *Kicking Away the Ladder*
David Brion Davis's *The Problem of Slavery in the Age of Revolution*
Milton Friedman's *The Role of Monetary Policy*
Milton Friedman's *Capitalism and Freedom*
David Graeber's *Debt: the First 5000 Years*
Friedrich Hayek's *The Road to Serfdom*
Karen Ho's *Liquidated: An Ethnography of Wall Street*

John Maynard Keynes's *The General Theory of Employment, Interest and Money*
Charles P. Kindleberger's *Manias, Panics and Crashes*
Robert Lucas's *Why Doesn't Capital Flow from Rich to Poor Countries?*
Burton G. Malkiel's *A Random Walk Down Wall Street*
Thomas Robert Malthus's *An Essay on the Principle of Population*
Karl Marx's *Capital*
Thomas Piketty's *Capital in the Twenty-First Century*
Amartya Sen's *Development as Freedom*
Adam Smith's *The Wealth of Nations*
Nassim Nicholas Taleb's *The Black Swan: The Impact of the Highly Improbable*
Amos Tversky's & Daniel Kahneman's *Judgment under Uncertainty: Heuristics and Biases*
Mahbub Ul Haq's *Reflections on Human Development*
Max Weber's *The Protestant Ethic and the Spirit of Capitalism*

FEMINISM AND GENDER STUDIES

Judith Butler's *Gender Trouble*
Simone De Beauvoir's *The Second Sex*
Michel Foucault's *History of Sexuality*
Betty Friedan's *The Feminine Mystique*
Saba Mahmood's *The Politics of Piety: The Islamic Revival and the Feminist Subject*
Joan Wallach Scott's *Gender and the Politics of History*
Mary Wollstonecraft's *A Vindication of the Rights of Woman*
Virginia Woolf's *A Room of One's Own*

GEOGRAPHY

The Brundtland Report's *Our Common Future*
Rachel Carson's *Silent Spring*
Charles Darwin's *On the Origin of Species*
James Ferguson's *The Anti-Politics Machine*
Jane Jacobs's *The Death and Life of Great American Cities*
James Lovelock's *Gaia: A New Look at Life on Earth*
Amartya Sen's *Development as Freedom*
Mathis Wackernagel & William Rees's *Our Ecological Footprint*

HISTORY

Janet Abu-Lughod's *Before European Hegemony*
Benedict Anderson's *Imagined Communities*
Bernard Bailyn's *The Ideological Origins of the American Revolution*
Hanna Batatu's *The Old Social Classes And The Revolutionary Movements Of Iraq*
Christopher Browning's *Ordinary Men: Reserve Police Batallion 101 and the Final Solution in Poland*
Edmund Burke's *Reflections on the Revolution in France*
William Cronon's *Nature's Metropolis: Chicago And The Great West*
Alfred W. Crosby's *The Columbian Exchange*
Hamid Dabashi's *Iran: A People Interrupted*
David Brion Davis's *The Problem of Slavery in the Age of Revolution*
Nathalie Zemon Davis's *The Return of Martin Guerre*
Jared Diamond's *Guns, Germs & Steel: the Fate of Human Societies*
Frank Dikotter's *Mao's Great Famine*
John W Dower's *War Without Mercy: Race And Power In The Pacific War*
W. E. B. Du Bois's *The Souls of Black Folk*
Richard J. Evans's *In Defence of History*
Lucien Febvre's *The Problem of Unbelief in the 16th Century*
Sheila Fitzpatrick's *Everyday Stalinism*

The Macat Library By Discipline

Eric Foner's *Reconstruction: America's Unfinished Revolution, 1863-1877*
Michel Foucault's *Discipline and Punish*
Michel Foucault's *History of Sexuality*
Francis Fukuyama's *The End of History and the Last Man*
John Lewis Gaddis's *We Now Know: Rethinking Cold War History*
Ernest Gellner's *Nations and Nationalism*
Eugene Genovese's *Roll, Jordan, Roll: The World the Slaves Made*
Carlo Ginzburg's *The Night Battles*
Daniel Goldhagen's *Hitler's Willing Executioners*
Jack Goldstone's *Revolution and Rebellion in the Early Modern World*
Antonio Gramsci's *The Prison Notebooks*
Alexander Hamilton, John Jay & James Madison's *The Federalist Papers*
Christopher Hill's *The World Turned Upside Down*
Carole Hillenbrand's *The Crusades: Islamic Perspectives*
Thomas Hobbes's *Leviathan*
Eric Hobsbawm's *The Age Of Revolution*
John A. Hobson's *Imperialism: A Study*
Albert Hourani's *History of the Arab Peoples*
Samuel P. Huntington's *The Clash of Civilizations and the Remaking of World Order*
C. L. R. James's *The Black Jacobins*
Tony Judt's *Postwar: A History of Europe Since 1945*
Ernst Kantorowicz's *The King's Two Bodies: A Study in Medieval Political Theology*
Paul Kennedy's *The Rise and Fall of the Great Powers*
Ian Kershaw's *The "Hitler Myth": Image and Reality in the Third Reich*
John Maynard Keynes's *The General Theory of Employment, Interest and Money*
Charles P. Kindleberger's *Manias, Panics and Crashes*
Martin Luther King Jr's *Why We Can't Wait*
Henry Kissinger's *World Order: Reflections on the Character of Nations and the Course of History*
Thomas Kuhn's *The Structure of Scientific Revolutions*
Georges Lefebvre's *The Coming of the French Revolution*
John Locke's *Two Treatises of Government*
Niccolò Machiavelli's *The Prince*
Thomas Robert Malthus's *An Essay on the Principle of Population*
Mahmood Mamdani's *Citizen and Subject: Contemporary Africa And The Legacy Of Late Colonialism*
Karl Marx's *Capital*
Stanley Milgram's *Obedience to Authority*
John Stuart Mill's *On Liberty*
Thomas Paine's *Common Sense*
Thomas Paine's *Rights of Man*
Geoffrey Parker's *Global Crisis: War, Climate Change and Catastrophe in the Seventeenth Century*
Jonathan Riley-Smith's *The First Crusade and the Idea of Crusading*
Jean-Jacques Rousseau's *The Social Contract*
Joan Wallach Scott's *Gender and the Politics of History*
Theda Skocpol's *States and Social Revolutions*
Adam Smith's *The Wealth of Nations*
Timothy Snyder's *Bloodlands: Europe Between Hitler and Stalin*
Sun Tzu's *The Art of War*
Keith Thomas's *Religion and the Decline of Magic*
Thucydides's *The History of the Peloponnesian War*
Frederick Jackson Turner's *The Significance of the Frontier in American History*
Odd Arne Westad's *The Global Cold War: Third World Interventions And The Making Of Our Times*

LITERATURE

Chinua Achebe's *An Image of Africa: Racism in Conrad's Heart of Darkness*
Roland Barthes's *Mythologies*
Homi K. Bhabha's *The Location of Culture*
Judith Butler's *Gender Trouble*
Simone De Beauvoir's *The Second Sex*
Ferdinand De Saussure's *Course in General Linguistics*
T. S. Eliot's *The Sacred Wood: Essays on Poetry and Criticism*
Zora Neale Huston's *Characteristics of Negro Expression*
Toni Morrison's *Playing in the Dark: Whiteness in the American Literary Imagination*
Edward Said's *Orientalism*
Gayatri Chakravorty Spivak's *Can the Subaltern Speak?*
Mary Wollstonecraft's *A Vindication of the Rights of Women*
Virginia Woolf's *A Room of One's Own*

PHILOSOPHY

Elizabeth Anscombe's *Modern Moral Philosophy*
Hannah Arendt's *The Human Condition*
Aristotle's *Metaphysics*
Aristotle's *Nicomachean Ethics*
Edmund Gettier's *Is Justified True Belief Knowledge?*
Georg Wilhelm Friedrich Hegel's *Phenomenology of Spirit*
David Hume's *Dialogues Concerning Natural Religion*
David Hume's *The Enquiry for Human Understanding*
Immanuel Kant's *Religion within the Boundaries of Mere Reason*
Immanuel Kant's *Critique of Pure Reason*
Søren Kierkegaard's *The Sickness Unto Death*
Søren Kierkegaard's *Fear and Trembling*
C. S. Lewis's *The Abolition of Man*
Alasdair MacIntyre's *After Virtue*
Marcus Aurelius's *Meditations*
Friedrich Nietzsche's *On the Genealogy of Morality*
Friedrich Nietzsche's *Beyond Good and Evil*
Plato's *Republic*
Plato's *Symposium*
Jean-Jacques Rousseau's *The Social Contract*
Gilbert Ryle's *The Concept of Mind*
Baruch Spinoza's *Ethics*
Sun Tzu's *The Art of War*
Ludwig Wittgenstein's *Philosophical Investigations*

POLITICS

Benedict Anderson's *Imagined Communities*
Aristotle's *Politics*
Bernard Bailyn's *The Ideological Origins of the American Revolution*
Edmund Burke's *Reflections on the Revolution in France*
John C. Calhoun's *A Disquisition on Government*
Ha-Joon Chang's *Kicking Away the Ladder*
Hamid Dabashi's *Iran: A People Interrupted*
Hamid Dabashi's *Theology of Discontent: The Ideological Foundation of the Islamic Revolution in Iran*
Robert Dahl's *Democracy and its Critics*
Robert Dahl's *Who Governs?*
David Brion Davis's *The Problem of Slavery in the Age of Revolution*

The Macat Library By Discipline

Alexis De Tocqueville's *Democracy in America*
James Ferguson's *The Anti-Politics Machine*
Frank Dikotter's *Mao's Great Famine*
Sheila Fitzpatrick's *Everyday Stalinism*
Eric Foner's *Reconstruction: America's Unfinished Revolution, 1863-1877*
Milton Friedman's *Capitalism and Freedom*
Francis Fukuyama's *The End of History and the Last Man*
John Lewis Gaddis's *We Now Know: Rethinking Cold War History*
Ernest Gellner's *Nations and Nationalism*
David Graeber's *Debt: the First 5000 Years*
Antonio Gramsci's *The Prison Notebooks*
Alexander Hamilton, John Jay & James Madison's *The Federalist Papers*
Friedrich Hayek's *The Road to Serfdom*
Christopher Hill's *The World Turned Upside Down*
Thomas Hobbes's *Leviathan*
John A. Hobson's *Imperialism: A Study*
Samuel P. Huntington's *The Clash of Civilizations and the Remaking of World Order*
Tony Judt's *Postwar: A History of Europe Since 1945*
David C. Kang's *China Rising: Peace, Power and Order in East Asia*
Paul Kennedy's *The Rise and Fall of Great Powers*
Robert Keohane's *After Hegemony*
Martin Luther King Jr.'s *Why We Can't Wait*
Henry Kissinger's *World Order: Reflections on the Character of Nations and the Course of History*
John Locke's *Two Treatises of Government*
Niccolò Machiavelli's *The Prince*
Thomas Robert Malthus's *An Essay on the Principle of Population*
Mahmood Mamdani's *Citizen and Subject: Contemporary Africa And The Legacy Of Late Colonialism*
Karl Marx's *Capital*
John Stuart Mill's *On Liberty*
John Stuart Mill's *Utilitarianism*
Hans Morgenthau's *Politics Among Nations*
Thomas Paine's *Common Sense*
Thomas Paine's *Rights of Man*
Thomas Piketty's *Capital in the Twenty-First Century*
Robert D. Putman's *Bowling Alone*
John Rawls's *Theory of Justice*
Jean-Jacques Rousseau's *The Social Contract*
Theda Skocpol's *States and Social Revolutions*
Adam Smith's *The Wealth of Nations*
Sun Tzu's *The Art of War*
Henry David Thoreau's *Civil Disobedience*
Thucydides's *The History of the Peloponnesian War*
Kenneth Waltz's *Theory of International Politics*
Max Weber's *Politics as a Vocation*
Odd Arne Westad's *The Global Cold War: Third World Interventions And The Making Of Our Times*

POSTCOLONIAL STUDIES

Roland Barthes's *Mythologies*
Frantz Fanon's *Black Skin, White Masks*
Homi K. Bhabha's *The Location of Culture*
Gustavo Gutiérrez's *A Theology of Liberation*
Edward Said's *Orientalism*
Gayatri Chakravorty Spivak's *Can the Subaltern Speak?*

PSYCHOLOGY

Gordon Allport's *The Nature of Prejudice*
Alan Baddeley & Graham Hitch's *Aggression: A Social Learning Analysis*
Albert Bandura's *Aggression: A Social Learning Analysis*
Leon Festinger's *A Theory of Cognitive Dissonance*
Sigmund Freud's *The Interpretation of Dreams*
Betty Friedan's *The Feminine Mystique*
Michael R. Gottfredson & Travis Hirschi's *A General Theory of Crime*
Eric Hoffer's *The True Believer: Thoughts on the Nature of Mass Movements*
William James's *Principles of Psychology*
Elizabeth Loftus's *Eyewitness Testimony*
A. H. Maslow's *A Theory of Human Motivation*
Stanley Milgram's *Obedience to Authority*
Steven Pinker's *The Better Angels of Our Nature*
Oliver Sacks's *The Man Who Mistook His Wife For a Hat*
Richard Thaler & Cass Sunstein's *Nudge: Improving Decisions About Health, Wealth and Happiness*
Amos Tversky's *Judgment under Uncertainty: Heuristics and Biases*
Philip Zimbardo's *The Lucifer Effect*

SCIENCE

Rachel Carson's *Silent Spring*
William Cronon's *Nature's Metropolis: Chicago And The Great West*
Alfred W. Crosby's *The Columbian Exchange*
Charles Darwin's *On the Origin of Species*
Richard Dawkin's *The Selfish Gene*
Thomas Kuhn's *The Structure of Scientific Revolutions*
Geoffrey Parker's *Global Crisis: War, Climate Change and Catastrophe in the Seventeenth Century*
Mathis Wackernagel & William Rees's *Our Ecological Footprint*

SOCIOLOGY

Michelle Alexander's *The New Jim Crow: Mass Incarceration in the Age of Colorblindness*
Gordon Allport's *The Nature of Prejudice*
Albert Bandura's *Aggression: A Social Learning Analysis*
Hanna Batatu's *The Old Social Classes And The Revolutionary Movements Of Iraq*
Ha-Joon Chang's *Kicking Away the Ladder*
W. E. B. Du Bois's *The Souls of Black Folk*
Émile Durkheim's *On Suicide*
Frantz Fanon's *Black Skin, White Masks*
Frantz Fanon's *The Wretched of the Earth*
Eric Foner's *Reconstruction: America's Unfinished Revolution, 1863-1877*
Eugene Genovese's *Roll, Jordan, Roll: The World the Slaves Made*
Jack Goldstone's *Revolution and Rebellion in the Early Modern World*
Antonio Gramsci's *The Prison Notebooks*
Richard Herrnstein & Charles A Murray's *The Bell Curve: Intelligence and Class Structure in American Life*
Eric Hoffer's *The True Believer: Thoughts on the Nature of Mass Movements*
Jane Jacobs's *The Death and Life of Great American Cities*
Robert Lucas's *Why Doesn't Capital Flow from Rich to Poor Countries?*
Jay Macleod's *Ain't No Makin' It: Aspirations and Attainment in a Low Income Neighborhood*
Elaine May's *Homeward Bound: American Families in the Cold War Era*
Douglas McGregor's *The Human Side of Enterprise*
C. Wright Mills's *The Sociological Imagination*

The Macat Library By Discipline

Thomas Piketty's *Capital in the Twenty-First Century*
Robert D. Putman's *Bowling Alone*
David Riesman's *The Lonely Crowd: A Study of the Changing American Character*
Edward Said's *Orientalism*
Joan Wallach Scott's *Gender and the Politics of History*
Theda Skocpol's *States and Social Revolutions*
Max Weber's *The Protestant Ethic and the Spirit of Capitalism*

THEOLOGY

Augustine's *Confessions*
Benedict's *Rule of St Benedict*
Gustavo Gutiérrez's *A Theology of Liberation*
Carole Hillenbrand's *The Crusades: Islamic Perspectives*
David Hume's *Dialogues Concerning Natural Religion*
Immanuel Kant's *Religion within the Boundaries of Mere Reason*
Ernst Kantorowicz's *The King's Two Bodies: A Study in Medieval Political Theology*
Søren Kierkegaard's *The Sickness Unto Death*
C. S. Lewis's *The Abolition of Man*
Saba Mahmood's *The Politics of Piety: The Islamic Revival and the Feminist Subject*
Baruch Spinoza's *Ethics*
Keith Thomas's *Religion and the Decline of Magic*

COMING SOON

Chris Argyris's *The Individual and the Organisation*
Seyla Benhabib's *The Rights of Others*
Walter Benjamin's *The Work Of Art in the Age of Mechanical Reproduction*
John Berger's *Ways of Seeing*
Pierre Bourdieu's *Outline of a Theory of Practice*
Mary Douglas's *Purity and Danger*
Roland Dworkin's *Taking Rights Seriously*
James G. March's *Exploration and Exploitation in Organisational Learning*
Ikujiro Nonaka's *A Dynamic Theory of Organizational Knowledge Creation*
Griselda Pollock's *Vision and Difference*
Amartya Sen's *Inequality Re-Examined*
Susan Sontag's *On Photography*
Yasser Tabbaa's *The Transformation of Islamic Art*
Ludwig von Mises's *Theory of Money and Credit*

Macat Disciplines

Access the greatest ideas and thinkers across entire disciplines, including

GLOBALIZATION

Arjun Appadurai's, *Modernity at Large: Cultural Dimensions of Globalisation*

James Ferguson's, *The Anti-Politics Machine*

Geert Hofstede's, *Culture's Consequences*

Amartya Sen's, *Development as Freedom*

Macat analyses are available from all good bookshops and libraries.

Access hundreds of analyses through one, multimedia tool.
Join free for one month **library.macat.com**

Macat Pairs

Analyse historical and modern issues from opposite sides of an argument. Pairs include:

HOW TO RUN AN ECONOMY

John Maynard Keynes's
The General Theory OF Employment, Interest and Money

Classical economics suggests that market economies are self-correcting in times of recession or depression, and tend toward full employment and output. But English economist John Maynard Keynes disagrees.

In his ground-breaking 1936 study *The General Theory*, Keynes argues that traditional economics has misunderstood the causes of unemployment. Employment is not determined by the price of labor; it is directly linked to demand. Keynes believes market economies are by nature unstable, and so require government intervention. Spurred on by the social catastrophe of the Great Depression of the 1930s, he sets out to revolutionize the way the world thinks

Milton Friedman's
The Role of Monetary Policy

Friedman's 1968 paper changed the course of economic theory. In just 17 pages, he demolished existing theory and outlined an effective alternate monetary policy designed to secure 'high employment, stable prices and rapid growth.'

Friedman demonstrated that monetary policy plays a vital role in broader economic stability and argued that economists got their monetary policy wrong in the 1950s and 1960s by misunderstanding the relationship between inflation and unemployment. Previous generations of economists had believed that governments could permanently decrease unemployment by permitting inflation—and vice versa. Friedman's most original contribution was to show that this supposed trade-off is an illusion that only works in the short term.

Macat analyses are available from all good bookshops and libraries.

Access hundreds of analyses through one, multimedia tool.
Join free for one month **library.macat.com**

Macat Disciplines

*Access the greatest ideas and thinkers
across entire disciplines, including*

THE FUTURE OF DEMOCRACY

Robert A. Dahl's, *Democracy and Its Critics*
Robert A. Dahl's, *Who Governs?*
Alexis De Toqueville's, *Democracy in America*
Niccolò Machiavelli's, *The Prince*
John Stuart Mill's, *On Liberty*
Robert D. Putnam's, *Bowling Alone*
Jean-Jacques Rousseau's, *The Social Contract*
Henry David Thoreau's, *Civil Disobedience*

Macat Disciplines

Access the greatest ideas and thinkers across entire disciplines, including

TOTALITARIANISM

Sheila Fitzpatrick's, *Everyday Stalinism*
Ian Kershaw's, *The "Hitler Myth"*
Timothy Snyder's, *Bloodlands*

Macat analyses are available from all good bookshops and libraries.

Access hundreds of analyses through one, multimedia tool.
Join free for one month **library.macat.com**

Macat Pairs

Analyse historical and modern issues from opposite sides of an argument. Pairs include:

RACE AND IDENTITY

Zora Neale Hurston's
Characteristics of Negro Expression

Using material collected on anthropological expeditions to the South, Zora Neale Hurston explains how expression in African American culture in the early twentieth century departs from the art of white America. At the time, African American art was often criticized for copying white culture. For Hurston, this criticism misunderstood how art works. European tradition views art as something fixed. But Hurston describes a creative process that is alive, ever-changing, and largely improvisational. She maintains that African American art works through a process called 'mimicry'—where an imitated object or verbal pattern, for example, is reshaped and altered until it becomes something new, novel—and worthy of attention.

Frantz Fanon's
Black Skin, White Masks

Black Skin, White Masks offers a radical analysis of the psychological effects of colonization on the colonized.

Fanon witnessed the effects of colonization first hand both in his birthplace, Martinique, and again later in life when he worked as a psychiatrist in another French colony, Algeria. His text is uncompromising in form and argument. He dissects the dehumanizing effects of colonialism, arguing that it destroys the native sense of identity, forcing people to adapt to an alien set of values—including a core belief that they are inferior. This results in deep psychological trauma.

Fanon's work played a pivotal role in the civil rights movements of the 1960s.

Macat analyses are available from all good bookshops and libraries.

Access hundreds of analyses through one, multimedia tool.
Join free for one month **library.macat.com**

Printed in the United States
by Baker & Taylor Publisher Services